A Workl

Living in the Family
of
Grace

Charles C. Bing

GraceLife

Living in the Family of Grace

Leader's Guide

You should read this Leader's Guide if you are leading another person or a group of people through this discipleship study. It is very important that you understand how this material is designed.

The Model Behind the Study

You may notice some differences in this course from other discipleship materials. This study is based on the complete picture of what a disciple is and not just what a disciple knows or does.

Christians agree that Jesus directed us to make disciples in Matthew 28:18-20. But making disciples means different things to different people. How can we know when we have made a disciple? Is a disciple simply someone who has passed a course, learned Bible doctrines, or reads the Bible regularly?

A survey of discipleship programs, courses, and books demonstrates the different understandings of what it means to make a disciple. Some are never clear in what they are trying to produce, and it quickly becomes evident that there are different ways to get there. Some material is weighted heavily towards knowing doctrine or the Bible, others toward disciplined habits such as prayer, Bible study, and witnessing, and others on relationships or character.

One element that seems consistently lacking in discipleship materials is proper motivation. Perhaps this is why many who pass discipleship courses fail to continue their discipleship commitments. Disciples must be motivated to pay the high cost Jesus attached to discipleship. Jesus often spoke of blessings, consolations, rewards, and eternal significance in discussions about discipleship. A properly motivated disciple will overcome all obstacles to his or her growth.

That is where grace comes in. The grace of God that brings us salvation motivates us with love and gratitude to follow Christ in discipleship. Many discipleship materials seem to miss a consistent application of the blessings of grace to the Christian's life and growth. Jesus not only incorporated grace in His discipleship teachings to motivate us to follow Him, He also spoke of the blessing of rewards and eternal significance, and a future accounting for our deeds at the Judgment Seat of Christ.

To make a disciple, we must begin with the end in mind. In Matthew 10:25, Jesus says, "It is enough for a disciple that he be like his teacher."

Our goal is to develop Christlikeness in the disciple that is grounded in and motivated by grace.

With this in mind, here is a four-part model for balanced discipleship:

1. What does God want me to become? This involves transformation as the disciple becomes more like Jesus in inner character.

2. What does God want me to know? Information in the form of doctrine and Bible knowledge is necessary to a godly life.

3. What does God want me to do? We can't have true discipleship without discipline, though we can have discipline without true discipleship. The focus here is on application of truth in life and behavior.

4. What does God want me to enjoy? Here is the motivation for ongoing discipleship as the disciple gains an eternal perspective through an appreciation of God's grace.

Discipleship is more than knowing and doing. It is knowing, and doing, and being for the right reasons. Those reasons are a Christian's response to God's grace. We know that we are producing disciples of Christ when we see people balanced in Christlikeness through transformation, information, application, and motivation. Such a disciple will reproduce similar disciples.

The Leader of the Study

The material is designed to be most useful in a one-to-one, small group, or class setting. This assumes that you as a leader are needed to initiate and facilitate discussion and to motivate those taking the course. It also assumes that you are further along in your Christian walk, especially in your understanding of God's grace and other major Bible teachings.

You should always be mindful of your role as a model and mentor in the discipleship relationship. Disciples will be influenced as much or more by your character and genuine concern for them as they will by the material itself.

The Users of the Study

New Christians. Not much Bible knowledge or Christian experience is taken for granted so that this material can be used to get new Christians started in the Christian life. Terms, Bible passages, and important theological issues are explained as simply as possible. The course will ground them in the principles of grace while also helping them establish important Christian practices including prayer, Bible study, worship, witness, service, and stewardship.

Ungrounded Christians. This study is also good for those who have been Christians for some time, but have not fully realized the role of grace in their lives. It will help them apply grace consistently in their thinking about salvation, growth, and discipleship. They also will gain a deeper understanding and appreciation for the purpose of the Gospel of John, Romans, and Jesus' teaching on discipleship commitments.

Growing Christians. Because of the focus on grace, this study will also challenge mature Christians to appreciate even more what God has done for them in the whole scope of their salvation from beginning to end. The section on discipleship will be especially relevant to them, because these discipleship issues face all Christians everyday. The study will also help more mature Christians communicate grace to others in ministry and other situations.

You will need wisdom in how to guide your particular participants through the study. You should be flexible enough to pursue a topic deeper when the participants are familiar with the subject, or to simplify the more difficult issues.

The Content of the Study

Part I - Getting into God's Family is designed to clarify the content of the gospel and explain clearly the condition for salvation. Confusion about the gospel often leads to confusion about the Christian life. Passages from the Gospel of John are used while important issues like faith and grace are explained. This section will be a simple review for some, but a challenge to others who may not be clear on issues relating to salvation.

Part II - Growing Deeper in God's Grace is designed to incorporate the truth of God's grace learned in salvation into the Christian life. Since Romans emphasizes grace and the Christian life more than any other Bible book, it forms the basis for this part of the study. A survey of Romans shows how grace gives us a new identity, power, and purpose in life.

Part III - Becoming a Disciple of Jesus Christ is designed to challenge every Christian to a greater commitment to Jesus Christ no matter where they are in their spiritual walk. It discusses key statements by Jesus that define and characterize disciples. Each of the seven lessons covers what God wants you to know, what God wants you to do, and what God wants you to enjoy. Christians will examine what a true disciple is and does as they are challenged to make commitments in their own lives.

The Format of the Study

Each of the three major parts (I, II, III) begins with a short introduction explaining what that major section is about. You can assign the introduction with the first lesson in each part.

Learn to use the "A Look Back" and "A Look Ahead" statements at the beginning of each lesson, as well as the review and the memory verses at the end.

The basic approach of each lesson is to have participants interact with Bible truth and its application to their lives. Use their written answers to prompt discussion. You should sense when to probe for more discussion than the questions require.

Inserted discussions titled "Please Explain" pursue important topics, controversial issues, and frequently asked questions without side-tracking the main study. If appropriate and helpful, you should pursue these discussions.

Most of the time the Bible passages are printed out for consistency and ease of use. Participants should be told to bring their Bibles for some of the questions and for further study. The translation used is the New King James Version.

The Use of the Study

Lessons are designed to be completed by participants on their own in an hour or two. Encourage people to mark the material with questions, highlights, and observations as they read and prepare so they can refer to these notes in discussion later. Each discipling session should take about an hour.

When meeting together, you should ask for observations or comments about what was presented and studied. It is your responsibility to help the participant think clearly and biblically by using guiding questions or comments. Seek to motivate others with encouraging and affirming responses. Do not dominate the discussion, but allow others to see and speak for themselves.

Finally, pray for every participant between sessions and include prayer in every session. God will bless you as you look to Him.

Introduction

Welcome, friend, to the adventure of a lifetime-and beyond!

We don't know exactly where you are on your journey toward God, so we'll have to start at the beginning — where everybody starts! But that is good, because the first steps you need to take will set the pace for the rest of the journey. Sometimes people don't take the time to get off to a good start, and that makes the rest of the trip more difficult.

This study guide will introduce you to the important concept of grace. When you understand how God relates to us through grace, and how we live out our lives through grace, you will experience a new freedom and motivation to live for God. Grace is the foundational principle of our relationship with God. Understand it and you will not only grow in your relationship to God, but you will also be spared many problems.

In this study guide, you will encounter amazing truths that you need to know. These truths about life and God's purpose for you come from God Himself through the Bible. The Bible is God's Word to us, and can be trusted in its truthfulness. It is divided into two main sections, the Old Testament (which covers the time before Jesus Christ) and the New Testament (which covers the time during and after Jesus Christ).

In Parts I and II of your study guide, we will discuss specific portions of two important New Testament books, John and Romans. They will introduce you to the adventure of God's new life. Then in Part III we will see how to respond to what God has done for us so that we can follow Jesus in a deeper way. We have printed out the Bible' s text to make it easier for you. You will notice that we take the time to explain the text instead of just mentioning it. This is the best way to get the most out of the Bible.

As you go through this study, you will notice references that have a form like this: John 3:16. This is an easy way to abbreviate the location of a Bible verse. John is the book, 3 is the chapter, and 16 is the verse number. So it means the book of John, chapter 3, the 16th verse. We will use this short form to avoid writing out complete references.

Proceed at whatever pace best fits your need, but the book is divided so that one study can be done at a sitting. We urge you to understand the main ideas of each lesson before proceeding to the next, because the ideas build on each other. We also encourage you to memorize the suggested verses at the end of each lesson.

Now, begin your great adventure!

Until all hear,

Charlie

Charles C. Bing
President, GraceLife Ministries

Part I: Getting into God's Family

Introduction

This first part of your adventure will help you understand God's truth about your eternal destiny. The Bible tells you how to know that you have eternal life. That is another way of saying, how to know that you are what the Bible considers a true Christian.

We better not assume too much about where you are in relation to God or what you understand about becoming a Christian. People who use this study guide come to it in many ways from a variety of backgrounds. Our goal is to let you see for yourself what the Bible says about what a true Christian is.

One thing is certain: Unless you know for sure where you stand with God, there will be little or no motivation and success in trying to live for Him. So let's make sure you have a clear understanding.

 Your Turn
There are many ways people define what it means to be a Christian. Write down your idea of what makes a person a true Christian.

_____

_____

Not all ideas about what it means to be a Christian can be supported by the Bible. The Bible describes what it means to be a Christian with terms like:
- born again
- redeemed
- having eternal life
- justified
- saved

Notice that none of these terms refers to a person's outward behavior or religious affiliations. Perhaps the easiest concept to understand is that of becoming a member of God's family. When you become a member of God's family, you are born again with eternal life as God's child. That is what a Christian is.

Although many people say that all people are God's children, that is not what the Bible teaches. The Bible teaches that all people are God's creations, but not all are His children. As you will see, the Bible teaches that we can only become a child of God by a second birth into His family.

One book of the Bible was written purposely to tell us how to become a child of God and have eternal life. That book is the Gospel of John, the fourth book in the New Testament. Let's review its message so that you can know for sure that you have eternal life.

Lesson 1: A Book About Salvation

A Look Ahead
The purpose of this lesson is to show how God made eternal life possible for us because of who Jesus is, what He did, and how we respond.

We will look at the New Testament book of the Gospel of John first, because of its stated purpose. This book was written by the Apostle John, one of Jesus Christ's original twelve followers. He states the purpose in John 20:31:
but these are written that you may believe that Jesus is the Christ, the Son of God, and that believing you may have life in His Name.

Your Turn
1. How would you explain the purpose of the Gospel of John according to this verse?

_____

_____

_____

John is the only book in the Bible that was written with the declared purpose of bringing people to believe in Jesus Christ as the Son of God so they can have eternal life. As an apostle, John has first-hand knowledge about Jesus and His teachings.

John's message to us is centered in a historical person, Jesus Christ, Whom he presents as God Himself in the very first verse of his book:
In the beginning was the Word, and the Word was with God, and the Word was God. (John 1:1)

Your Turn
2. What three things does this verse tell us about Jesus Christ?

1. _____

2. _____

3. _____

John calls Jesus Christ the "Word" because Jesus is God's message to us. From the beginning of time, Jesus was "with God" but also "was God." Of course, Jesus remains fully God today.

Please Explain...

What is meant by eternal life?

Eternal life is simply God's life given to us. It is eternal because God is eternal. But it is more than just a duration of time after we die. The Bible teaches that eternal life begins with a relationship with God and His Son, Jesus Christ: "And this is eternal life, that they may know You, the only true God, and Jesus Christ whom you have sent" (John 17:3). Eternal life becomes ours as soon as we are born into God's family. Notice how eternal life is promised as a present possession in this verse: "Most assuredly, I say to you, he who hears My word and believes in Him who sent Me has everlasting life, and shall not come into judgment, but has passed from death into life" (John 5:24). When God's life is present in ours, we can also enjoy the fullness of life. Jesus called it an abundant life (John 10:10). So eternal life is not only defined by quantity of life after we die, but also by quality of life while we live.

The Bible teaches that there is one God revealed to us as three persons: God the Father, God the Son, and God the Holy Spirit. Each person of this "Trinity" is equal and fully God. Jesus not only claimed to be God, but he did things only God could do, such as forgive sins, control nature, and create things. His followers addressed Him with divine titles like "Son of God," "Messiah," "Lord," and "God." As God the Son, Jesus represents God the Father to us. As God the Holy Spirit, He gives new birth and lives in those who are God's children.

This idea of a Trinity is difficult to fully explain and understand given our human limitations. Every illustration ultimately falls short. One illustration of the three-in-one concept is a man who is a father, a son, and a husband. Though he is one man, he functions in three different roles, depending on the relationship in view. Water is another illustration in that it can be liquid, solid (ice), or gas (steam). Some find this diagram helpful:

Jesus did what only God could do:

He was in the beginning with God. All things were made through Him, and without Him nothing was made that was made. In Him was life, and the life was the Light of men. (John 1:2-4)

Your Turn

3. What is the main truth taught about Jesus Christ in these verses?

_____

_____

_____

_____

Jesus Christ is our Creator who came to give us God's own life. It would be foolish, wouldn't it, to think that we could live a full life or have eternal life without the Originator of life? Yet John tells us that many rejected Jesus' offer of eternal life, even his own Jewish people:

He was in the world, and the world was made through Him, and the world did not know Him. He came to His own, and His own did not receive Him. (John 1:10-11)

Though He was rejected by most, those who accept His offer find a new way of relating to God. He makes them His children!

But as many as received Him, to them He gave the right to become children of God, to those who believe in His Name. (John 1:12)

Your Turn

4. According to this verse, how can a person become a child of God?

_____

_____

_____

_____

_____

In contrast to those who did not accept the truth about Jesus Christ, some will "receive" or accept that truth. The word "right" shows that this extraordinary privilege of becoming God's child is granted to us by His divine authority. "His Name" means all that He stands for, which as explained so far, includes His divine character and life. When we believe in His Name, we accept who He claims to be.

Your Turn

5. It is important to understand exactly what faith is, since that is our only condition for receiving eternal life. Does the definition in "Please Explain" differ from what you thought or heard before? How?

_____

_____

_____

_____

How can faith alone be enough to save us? Because our salvation comes to us by God's grace. Jesus has revealed that grace to us. Circle the word grace when it appears in this passage.

And the Word became flesh and dwelt among us, and we beheld His glory, the glory as of the only begotten of the Father, full of grace and truth. John bore witness of Him and cried out, saying, "This was He of whom I said, 'He who comes after me is preferred before me, for He was before me.' And of His fullness we have all received, and grace for grace. For the law was given through Moses; but grace and truth came through Jesus Christ. No one has seen God at any time. The only begotten Son, who is in the bosom of the Father, He has declared Him." (John 1:14-18)

God the Son became a man with a real human body. He was born to a woman and was named Jesus. He became fully human (for example, He hungered, thirsted, and experienced emotions), but remained fully God also. We see from the story of His life in the Bible that He was full of grace and truth just as John describes. He not only embodied truth, He taught truths we needed to know, such as: We are sinners who need to be saved, God loves us and has provided a Savior, and we can be saved through faith in His Son. He was also full of grace, seen in His gracious attitudes and actions towards the people He met. Because of His truth and grace, we are able to understand what God the Father is like. Jesus makes Him known to us.

Please Explain...

What does it mean to believe?

The Gospel of John that you are studying uses believe almost 100 times, most often as the condition for obtaining eternal life. Interestingly, the noun form of believe, faith, is not used at all. To believe means simply to be persuaded that something is true. In other words, we accept the truthfulness of a fact or a statement. When used in the Bible to explain how a person can become a child of God, believe means to be persuaded that Jesus' promise of eternal life is true because He died for our sins and rose from the dead. We either believe this or we do not. It is not how we believe (that is, the quality or quantity of our faith), but what or who we believe in, that saves us. For example, if you believe a doctor's directions, you will take the medicine he prescribes. Whether you have little or great faith in his words, the medicine will have the same effect on you.

Belief should be distinguished from obedience to God's commands or from any commitment we make to God. These things are the results of believing, but are not a part of believing itself. It is by only believing in Jesus Christ alone that a person becomes a child of God.

What is grace?

In the New Testament, grace comes from the same word that means "gift." Grace, then, is always a free gift. When we talk about the grace of God towards us, we can define it as God's undeserved favor given to sinners. Notice what is stated or implied in this definition:

- It comes from God as a reflection of His character.

- It is undeserved. We cannot earn it (or it would be a payment, not a gift).

- It is to our favor, or benefit and blessing.

- It is given as a gift, not a debt or payment or obligation. It is absolutely free.

- It is for sinners who only deserve God's justice and punishment.

Grace is the opposite of obligation. It is never owed. It is only given because of the good will of the giver. The Bible always presents eternal salvation as a free gift of grace. We can never earn grace, and God is never obligated to give us His grace because of what we do. Furthermore, grace is not God's enablement to help us earn salvation. It is the gift of salvation itself. In another New Testament book, we read "For by grace you have been saved through faith, and that not of yourselves; it is the gift of God, not of works, lest anyone should boast" (Ephesians 2:8-9). God can give us His grace freely because He paid a high price for our salvation, a price that we could never pay — His only Son, Jesus Christ. Jesus was hung on a cross until He died. In His death He paid the penalty for our sins, though He was innocent. You will read more about this later.

Your Turn

6. Using what we have learned so far, summarize how Jesus Christ is God's grace to us.

_____

_____

_____

_____

_____

The law reflects various aspects of the character of God and shows us that as sinners we fall far short of His character. We can never achieve His perfect standard. Therefore, the law keeps people under condemnation. It also keeps people living in insecurity about their relationship with God, because they know they cannot perform flawlessly. The law acts as an external force that governs external behavior, but it cannot change the heart.

Your Turn

7. To understand the impossibility of keeping the law perfectly, do this check-up on yourself. The most familiar part of the law is called the Ten Commandments (found in Exodus 20:1-17). Jesus explained some of them to mean not only the outward act, but the inner attitude. Check the laws you think you have broken either by action or attitude.

___ "You shall have no other gods before Me." Since God is more important than anything or anyone else, you have always given Him your full devotion.

___ "You shall not make for yourself any carved image." You have never represented God as any less than He is by images, pictures, or inadequate concepts about Him.

___ "You shall not take the name of the Lord your God in vain." You have never lowered God's reputation by careless references to Him.

___ "Remember the Sabbath day, to keep it holy." You have always given God the faithful regular worship He desires.

___ "Honor your father and your mother." In your attitudes and actions you have always shown respect for your parents.

___ "You shall not murder." You have never taken another's life, or even hated another person, which is "mental murder."

___ "You shall not commit adultery." You have been faithful to your marriage partner or the partner of another person even in your emotions and thoughts.

___ "You shall not steal." You have always respected the right of others to have their own possessions.

___ "You shall not bear false witness." You have been always totally honest and truthful.

___ "You shall not covet your neighbor's [possessions]." You have been always content with what you have so that you have never wished less for anyone else.

If you checked any of the above (and we all will!), the bad news is that we have failed to keep God's law, which shows we deserve His punishment. However, the good news is that God has provided His Son to take in our place the punishment that we deserve!

So, grace is contrary to the law. Grace based on truth assures us of God's unconditional pardon. It gives us His unconditional acceptance. It moves our hearts to live for God, not because we want to earn His blessing, but because He has already blessed us by His grace. This is the basic difference from living under the law. The law said to obey and you will be blessed; Grace says you are blessed, therefore obey. The law says "Do;" grace says "Done!"

Our birth into God's family is not by our efforts any more than our physical birth was by our efforts. In both our physical birth and spiritual birth, the birth starts and ends with the efforts of someone else. That is what John means when he says, *who were born, not of blood, nor of the will of the flesh, nor of the will of man, but of God.* (John 1:13)

Now that you understand that becoming a Christian means becoming a child of God through faith in Jesus Christ, you should recognize that there are many false views of how to become a Christian.

Your Turn

8. Explain what is wrong with each of these false views of how a person becomes a Christian.

Keeping religious rules or laws. _____

_____

Participating in rituals, like communion or baptism. _____

_____

Joining a church or any other group. _____

_____

Please Explain...

What is meant by the law?

John's original readers included people of Jewish background who were familiar with life under the many laws that God gave to them through Moses. (The story of how the law was given is found in Exodus 19-20 in the Old Testament.) The law has hundreds of requirements to govern behavior toward God and toward other people. To disobey or break the law resulted in God's punishment. Of course, no one could keep all the laws perfectly then or now, so ultimately the law only condemns us by showing us our sinfulness and imperfection. In this way, however, the law leads us to accept God's way of salvation by grace through faith in Jesus Christ. Jesus is the only One perfect enough to fulfill all the requirements of the law for us, because He Himself never sinned nor could He sin. Then He died as a perfect sacrifice for our sins, and in so doing, did what we could never do.

Living in a "Christian" culture, like the United States. _____

_____

Reforming outward behavior. _____

_____

Reading the Bible. _____

_____

Making a commitment to serve God or to submit to God as the Master of your life, or as some would say "Make Him Lord of all of your life." _____

_____

Turning from all sins and feeling sorry for sins. _____

_____

Notice that all of the above are contrary to the freeness of grace. A person becomes a child of God through faith alone in Jesus Christ alone. It is that simple! It is simple because God did all the work. There is nothing left for us to do but accept it. This is what distinguishes biblical Christianity from every other religion in the world. In every other religion you must do something to earn God's favor. In biblical Christianity, everything has been done. All we must do is accept what God has done for us in providing eternal life through Jesus Christ.

 Points to Remember

- God the Son became a man named Jesus Christ.

- Jesus came to give us God's eternal life now and for all eternity.

- We cannot earn eternal life by good behavior, by doing good deeds, or by doing anything.

- We must accept his offer of eternal life by believing in the person, provision, and promise of Jesus Christ.

- When we believe, we become a member of God's family.

Your Turn

9. As you review John 1:1-18, you see how Jesus is described and that people can respond to Him in different ways. Put into words your understanding of who Jesus is and how you have responded to His promise to make you a member of God's family.

_____

_____

_____

_____

_____

Take It to Heart
Memorize these verses:

John 1:12 *But as many as received Him, to them He gave the right to become children of God, to those who believe in His Name.*

John 1:14 *And the Word became flesh and dwelt among us, and we beheld His glory, the glory as of the only begotten of the Father, full of grace and truth.*

In the next lesson, you will read about a religious man who still needs to know how to have eternal life. Jesus tells him how with an extraordinary statement.

Lesson 2: A Story about Salvation

A Look Back
Review what a true Christian is and recite the two memory verses from the previous lesson.

A Look Ahead
We will learn more about the simple condition of salvation by studying a story of a religious man who needed eternal life.

In the last lesson you learned how simple it is to become a member of God's family because of God's grace. Though it is simple, it may not be easy, because it depends on trusting in what Jesus has done instead of what you can do.

Your Turn
1. List some of the accomplishments, achievements, positions, titles, awards, or religious recognitions that you have acquired in this life.

_____

_____

How do you think God views your accomplishments?

_____

_____

John's Gospel has an interesting story that shows how anyone can become a member of God's family. In John 3 Jesus spoke to a religious leader named Nicodemus:

There was a man of the Pharisees named Nicodemus, a ruler of the Jews. This man came to Jesus by night and said to Him, "Rabbi, we know that You are a teacher come from God; for no one can do these signs that You do unless God is with him." Jesus answered and said to him, "Most assuredly, I say to you, unless one is born again, he cannot see the kingdom of God." Nicodemus said to Him, "How can a man be born when he is old? Can he enter a second time into his mother's womb and be born?" Jesus answered, "Most assuredly, I say to you, unless one is born of water and the Spirit, he cannot enter the kingdom of God. That which is born of the flesh is flesh, and that which is born of the Spirit is spirit. Do not marvel that I said to you, 'You must be born again.'" (John 3:1-7)

As a prestigious religious leader and teacher in Israel, Nicodemus was perhaps reluctant to be seen with the controversial Jesus, so he approached Him at night. Though he only declares that Jesus is a "teacher come from God," Nicodemus was evidently searching for the truth about how to obtain eternal life. The "kingdom of God" refers to the kingdom that Jesus will rule over when He returns. Only those with eternal life will be able to enter it. Jesus answers the question of Nicodemus's heart by telling him he "must be born again." Jesus refers here to the new life that God's Spirit begins in us.

Your Turn
2. How did Nicodemus misunderstand what Jesus said about a new birth?

_____

_____

_____

Nicodemus did not understand that Jesus was talking about a spiritual birth. That is why Jesus says we must be "born of water and of the Spirit." Water is a familiar symbol in the Bible for the Holy Spirit. Jesus was simply saying that a person had to be born of the Holy Spirit.

This new birth is not by any visible means, like water baptism. Jesus described the Holy Spirit's invisible work this way:
"The wind blows where it wishes, and you hear the sound of it, but cannot tell where it comes from and where it goes. So is everyone who is born of the Spirit." (John 3:8)

Though we know the wind blows, we do not know everything about it, like its origin and final destination. Likewise, we know we are born again through faith in Christ, though we may not know everything about how God invisibly brings us into His family. There is an element of mystery with both the wind and the new birth, but they are real!

To show the simplicity of how salvation can be obtained, Jesus reminded Nicodemus of an Old Testament story that would have been familiar to him. The story is found in Numbers 21:4-9.
Then they [the Israelites] journeyed from Mount Hor by the Way of the Red Sea, to go around the land of Edom; and the soul of the people became very discouraged on the way. And the people spoke against God and against Moses: "Why have you brought us up out of Egypt to die in the wilderness? For there is no food and no water, and our soul loathes this worthless bread." So the Lord sent fiery serpents among the people, and they bit the

Perhaps you noticed that Jesus never tells Nicodemus that he must repent. In fact, John never mentions the words *repent* or *repentance* in his book. That certainly emphasizes the freeness of the offer of eternal life by simply believing.

Repent or *repentance* basically means to have a change of mind or heart. But it must always be interpreted in its context as to how it is used. Repentance is not used in the New Testament to speak of an outward turning from sin or change of conduct. Rather, it speaks of the inner change which should logically and naturally produce such outer changes (See Luke 3:8; Acts 26:20). Understood in this way, repentance is not adding works or self-reformation as another condition for eternal salvation.

Sometimes it appears that repentance was used by Jesus in the gospels to remind the Jewish people of their relationship to God governed by the law which required repentance for God's blessing. It was also the way for Jews to escape God's judgment on that generation which rejected Christ (See Luke 10:13-14; 13:1-5; Acts 2:38).

When Jesus and other New Testament writers seem to speak of repentance in relation to eternal salvation, it is in no case a second condition that must be added to believing for salvation. *Believe* is the way the condition is normally stated, but at times, *repentance* seems to be used as a synonym for believing (For example, see Luke 16:30; Acts 17:30, 34; 20:21; 2 Peter 3:9). When it is used this way, it refers to the change of heart about one's

continued on page 21

people; and many of the people of Israel died. Therefore the people came to Moses, and said, "We have sinned, for we have spoken against the LORD and against you; pray to the LORD that He take away the serpents from us." So Moses prayed for the people. Then the LORD said to Moses, "Make a fiery serpent, and set it on a pole; and it shall be that everyone who is bitten, when he looks at it, shall live." So Moses made a bronze serpent, and put it on a pole; and so it was, if a serpent had bitten anyone, when he looked at the bronze serpent, he lived.*

Your Turn
3. In this story, what did Moses have to do for the people?

_____

_____

_____

_____

What did the people have to do to be saved from death?

_____

_____

_____

_____

Referring to this story, Jesus said to Nicodemus,
"And as Moses lifted up the serpent in the wilderness, even so must the Son of Man be lifted up, that whoever believes in Him should not perish but have eternal life." (John 3:14-15)

Your Turn
4. What was Jesus saying the only thing Nicodemus (and we) need to do to be saved?

_____

_____

_____

_____

The only thing necessary for the Israelites was to look. It was a look of faith. God did not require the people to do any work or to earn their healing in any way. Similarly, Jesus did not tell Nicodemus to study harder, become a better person, make any commitments to serve Him, or obey any commands. By reminding Nicodemus of this story, Jesus was showing him that the new birth (becoming a member of God's family, obtaining God's eternal life) is by only looking to Him, that is, believing in Him.

The verse that summarizes Jesus' message to Nicodemus (and us!) best is a familiar one to many because it so clearly captures the central truth of God's promise of salvation:
"For God so loved the world that He gave His only begotten Son, that whosoever believes in Him should not perish, but have everlasting life." (John 3:16)

Your Turn
5. In John 3:16 the exceeding great love of God is declared for us. What do you see in this verse that emphasizes God's love for us?

_____

_____

_____

_____

_____

_____

What is the only condition for salvation according to this verse?

_____

_____

Jesus had to die as a payment for our sin that separates us from God. In His justice, God must punish all sin. Since Jesus is God the Son, His death on the cross was payment sufficient enough for anyone and everyone regardless of race, color, religion, nationality, or degree of sinfulness. Because Jesus rose from the dead three days after His death, we know that God accepted Jesus' sacrifice. He is a living Savior! That means He will fulfill His promise of salvation for us today if we believe in who He is and what He did for us.

Please Explain...
What about repentance?
continued from page 20

needy condition before God and God's provision for that need, just as faith in Jesus Christ also implies that one has changed his mind about his relationship to God.

Keep in mind there is occasionally an overlap in the ideas of repentance and faith in Christ. But repentance is the more general term and may not always include the specific faith that brings eternal life. A person can repent of many things, and never believe in Jesus Christ as Savior.

So now, friend, can you see how your eternal salvation (your membership in God's family) is by His grace and not your effort? Yes, believing is simple, but not easy. Some people find it hard to believe.

Your Turn

6. Why do you think some people find it hard to believe that eternal life is a free gift?

_____

_____

_____

_____

_____

It may be hard to believe that so much can be yours without doing something to deserve it. But that is God's grace! God only offers salvation as a free gift so that He alone will be glorified (receive the credit), not us.

Understanding this concept of God's grace is crucial to living the rest of your life for God. Grace is not only the chief principle by which we are saved, it continues to be the chief principle for living and enjoying the Christian life. When properly understood, grace will motivate you to honor God with your life because He has been so good to you.

You can see how grace is the chief distinctive of biblical Christianity. Grace means that we have unconditional acceptance from God. He will always love us regardless of our performance, because we are His children.

Points to Remember

— God loves you.

— God gave His only Son, Jesus, to die as payment for your sins and he rose from the dead.

— Jesus now lives and offers eternal life by new birth into God's family to all who believe in His person, provision, and promise.

— God's grace is the basis of this salvation, not anything that we can do.

Your Turn

7. Have you experienced God's grace through a new birth into His family? Remember, you become a member of God's family by believing that Jesus Christ will give you eternal life because He died to pay the penalty for your sins and rose from the dead. If you have believed this, write out a short prayer to God that expresses your faith in Christ as your Savior.

_____

_____

_____

_____

Now go back and look at the beginning of Part I when you wrote what you thought a Christian is. How has your thinking changed because of this study?

_____

_____

_____

Take It to Heart

Memorize these verses:

John 3:3 *Jesus answered and said to him, "Most assuredly, I say to you, unless one is born again, he cannot see the kingdom of God."*

John 3:16 *For God so loved the world that He gave His only begotten Son, that whoever believes in Him should not perish, but have everlasting life.*

You've finished Part I! But you have only begun to discover what it means to be a member of God's family. In Part II, you will learn the most important truths in the Bible about your new life.

Part II: Growing Deeper in God's Grace

Introduction

As a member of God's family, God wants you to grow as His child. The second part of our study will help you get off to a healthy start by giving you greater insight into what has happened to make you a part of God's family. You will also grow in your appreciation of the greatness of God's amazing grace. You will see how grace is not only the basis of your salvation, but also the basis of your Christian life and growth as a child of God. By the end of Part II you will understand that grace makes it possible to know beyond any doubt that you are saved and eternally secure in God's family.

 Your Turn

Before we start, go back and review the meaning of grace on page 14. Write out a good definition here.

A Book about Grace

To better appreciate grace, we will look at a New Testament book that explains our salvation and our Christian life from the viewpoint of grace. That book is Romans. Just as John emphasized believing, so Romans emphasizes grace. (Romans mentions grace more than any other New Testament book.) Romans shows how God's grace that was first experienced in salvation continues into the Christian's life.

To introduce us to its contents, the writer of Romans (the Apostle Paul) states its main theme in the first chapter.
For I am not ashamed of the gospel of Christ, for it is the power of God to salvation for everyone who believes, for the Jew first and also for the Greek. For in it the righteousness of God is revealed... (Romans 1:16-17a)

The word "gospel" literally means "good news," and here refers to the offer of salvation from beginning to end through faith in the person, provision, and promise of Jesus Christ. This reasserts what John's book has already shown us: that the gospel is God's way of salvation to anyone who believes. The gospel reveals God's righteousness and makes it possible for us to be declared righteous also. Once we are declared righteous, we can, by the same power, be saved from the effects and consequences of sin in this life which in turn affects our rewards and experience in the future kingdom of Jesus Christ. To be saved means to be delivered from something. Now that we have been delivered from the penalty of sin (eternal death), we need to be delivered from the power of sin in our daily lives.

After the introduction, the body of the book of Romans moves very logically to discuss these subjects in this order: sin, salvation, sanctification, security, selection, and service. These words may not mean very much to you now, but they will as you read on.

Lesson 3: God's Grace and Our Sin

A Look Back
Explain why you believe you are a Christian. Recite the two memory verses from the previous lesson.

A Look Ahead
In this lesson we will see why we needed God's grace.

The main body of Romans begins with the declaration that all human beings in their unsaved state are under the wrath of God.

For the wrath of God is revealed from heaven against all ungodliness and unrighteousness of men, who suppress the truth in unrighteousness.
(Romans 1:18)

Your Turn
1. The word "wrath" refers to God's just anger towards sin. Notice that this statement is in the present tense. How do you see God's anger toward sin displayed in the consequences of sin people might experience today? How do you think God's anger toward sin will be displayed in eternity?

Because we were all sinners under God's wrath, we could not experience His abundant life now or for eternity. We deserved this wrath because we were ungodly (not like God) and unrighteous (unacceptable to God because of our sin). The only way to escape God's wrath was to have our ungodliness and unrighteousness removed.

Before he tells us how God has provided for our ungodliness and unrighteousness to be removed, the writer wants to be sure that we understand there are no exceptions to this unrighteousness. We were all guilty. The spiritual history of all humanity shows that as a whole we had ignored God and turned from Him to live degrading lives of sin:

because what may be known of God is manifest in them, for God has shown it to them. For since the creation of the world His invisible attributes are clearly seen, being understood by the things that are made, even His eternal power and Godhead, so that they are without excuse, because, although they knew God, they did not glorify Him as God, nor were thankful, but became futile in their thoughts, and their foolish hearts were darkened. Professing to be wise, they became fools, and changed the glory of the incorruptible God into an image made like corruptible man—and birds and four-footed animals and creeping things.

Therefore God also gave them up to uncleanness, in the lusts of their hearts, to dishonor their bodies among themselves, who exchanged the truth of God for the lie, and worshiped and served the creature rather than the Creator, who is blessed forever. Amen.

For this reason God gave them up to vile passions. For even their women exchanged the natural use for what is against nature. Likewise also the men, leaving the natural use of the woman, burned in their lust for one another, men with men committing what is shameful, and receiving in themselves the penalty of their error which was due.

And even as they did not like to retain God in their knowledge, God gave them over to a debased mind, to do those things which are not fitting. (Romans 1:19-28)

Your Turn

2. According to this passage, what has been humanity's response to God's revelation of Himself in creation?

_____

_____

_____

_____

How is God's response to humanity described?

_____

_____

_____

_____

Please Explain...

What is death?

While many think of death as cessation of life, it is better to think of it as separation from life. The Bible speaks of physical death, spiritual death, and eternal death. When we die physically, our bodies separate from our life-giving spirits, yet the spirit goes on to exist eternally and is eventually reunited with the body. So once born, a person never ceases to exist. The only question is whether he or she exists forever as a resurrected person in God's presence (eternal life) or exists forever separated from God (eternal death). This is why a person who is alive physically can be called dead spiritually. That person is separated from God by his or her unbelief. We are all separated from God in this life and the next unless we believe in Jesus Christ's offer of eternal life. Death first came through Adam, the first man. God warned that if he ate the forbidden fruit he would die. Adam ate, but he did not die physically at that time. He did, however, die spiritually by being separated immediately from God in his experience so that he even hid from God. The story of Adam's sin and its horrible consequences is in Genesis 2 and 3.

The phrase "God gave them up" (or "over"), which appears three times, refers to God's judgment of letting people run the course of their sin and suffer the consequences. Some of the consequences are listed in the next verses:
being filled with all unrighteousness, sexual immorality, wickedness, covetousness, maliciousness; full of envy, murder, strife, deceit, evil-mindedness; they are whisperers, backbiters, haters of God, violent, proud, boasters, inventors of evil things, disobedient to parents, undiscerning, untrustworthy, unloving, unforgiving, unmerciful. (Romans 1:29-31)

These negative things are evidence of our sinful motives that bring God's wrath. This sinfulness shows that we deserve death. That is why the writer concludes this passage by saying,
who, knowing the righteous judgment of God, that those who practice such things are deserving of death, not only do the same but also approve of those who practice them. (Romans 1:32)

 Your Turn

3. How would you explain to a non-believing friend, who feels very much alive, that he or she is spiritually dead?

_____

_____

_____

_____

_____

The writer of Romans sums up his discussion of our sin by concluding that every single person in the world is guilty of sin before God. As you read the passage below, circle the words that indicate these statements include each and every human being.

What then? Are we better than they? Not at all. For we have previously
charged both Jews and Greeks that they are all under sin.

>*As it is written:*
>*"There is none righteous, no, not one;*
>*There is none who understands;*
>*There is none who seeks after God.*
>*They have all turned aside;*
>*They have together become unprofitable;*
>*There is none who does good, no, not one."*
>*"Their throat is an open tomb;*
>*With their tongues they have practiced deceit;"*
>*"The poison of asps is under their lips;"*
>*"Whose mouth is full of cursing and bitterness."*
>*"Their feet are swift to shed blood;*
>*Destruction and misery are in their ways;*
>*And the way of peace they have not known."*
>*"There is no fear of God before their eyes."*

Now we know that whatever the law says, it says to those who are under
the law, that every mouth may be stopped, and all the world may become
guilty before God. (Romans 3:9-19)

The conclusion is that even the Jews, God's chosen people, are as guilty as
the non-Jews, or Gentiles. As if giving a physical examination from the head
to the toes, the writer shows from this spiritual examination that sin has so
infected human beings that on our own we can say nothing in our defense:
"that every mouth may be stopped." Without Jesus Christ we all stand silently
guilty before God knowing we have earned a well-deserved punishment. Sin is
that which falls short of God's righteousness. It is a transgression of His stan-
dards and laws. In its essence, sin is an anti-God attitude or action. As sinners
we have broken God's laws and must therefore be punished with separation
from God in this life and in eternity.

Your Turn
**4. Think of the best and most moral person you know,
one you would not hesitate to call good. Why could this
person not have eternal life without Jesus Christ?**

What Romans shows is that because sin so infects humanity, our own efforts cannot make us acceptable to God. Doing good does not cure being bad. We must be declared righteous by God. The conclusion to this section about our sin follows:

Therefore by the deeds of the law no flesh will be justified in His sight, for by the law is the knowledge of sin. (Romans 3:20)

"Deeds of the law" refers to those things that God commands and we might do, however good, to try to earn God's acceptance. But here we see that the purpose of the law is not to make us acceptable to God (that is, "justified," which will be explained in Lesson 4).

 Your Turn

5. **According to Romans 3:20, what is the purpose of the law?**

_____

_____

_____

The law is like a doctor's X-ray machine. The X-ray does not cure us, it shows us what is wrong. But when we know what is wrong, our sense of need drives us to seek the proper cure. In the same way, the law shows us that we are sinners so that we might seek God's righteousness as a gift of grace, not something we must earn.

 Your Turn

6. **Review how the law exposed sin in the exercise using the Ten Commandments (Part I, Lesson 1, pp. 14-15). Do you think anyone would get a perfect score? Why or why not? If you think they would, read Matthew 5:21-48 to see how Jesus interpreted some of these laws. Write your thoughts below.**

_____

_____

_____

_____

_____

_____

Dear friend, perhaps you have not fully realized that without God's righteousness, you are in a sinful state before God. Can you now see that you are not good enough and can never do enough good deeds to get into God's family? Have you believed in Jesus Christ as your Savior who will forgive your sin and replace it with God's righteousness? If you have not, why not pause right now and settle this important issue, then take time to thank God for giving you eternal life through Jesus Christ?

Points to Remember

— We are all sinners under God's wrath.

— We all need God's righteousness to escape His wrath.

— We can not obtain God's righteousness by our efforts or good works.

Your Turn

7. To see what you understand about what Romans has said about sin, write down what you would say to a basically moral person, who does not think he or she is a very bad sinner, to convince them that they are a sinner in need of God's righteousness.

_____

_____

_____

_____

_____

Take It to Heart
Memorize these verses:
Romans 1:16 _For I am not ashamed of the gospel of Christ, for it is the power of God to salvation for everyone who believes, for the Jew first and also for the Greek._

Romans 3:20 _Therefore by the deeds of the law no flesh will be justified in His sight, for by the law is the knowledge of sin._

Please continue to the next lesson in this study guide. It will help you understand even more how God has wonderfully provided for your salvation!

Lesson 4: God's Grace and Our Salvation

 A Look Back
Explain why we need God's righteousness and recite the two memory verses from the previous lesson.

A Look Ahead
In this lesson you will see how God solved our sin problem and provided salvation with all its blessings.

After painting such a dark background of sin in Romans 1:18—3:20, it is a welcome relief for Romans to bring us the bright good news of God's salvation. If we cannot obtain God's righteousness by our efforts or by the law, then how can we obtain it?

The words "But now" in our next passage in Romans signal the great shift and contrast from the discussion of our sin to the discussion of our salvation: *But now the righteousness of God apart from the law is revealed, being witnessed by the Law and the Prophets, even the righteousness of God, through faith in Jesus Christ, to all and on all who believe. For there is no difference; for all have sinned and fall short of the glory of God, being justified freely by His grace through the redemption that is in Christ Jesus.* (Romans 3:21-24)

Your Turn
1. According to these verses, how can we obtain God's righteousness?

Who can obtain God's righteousness? _____

The simplicity of God's offer is so profound that the author repeats the idea of faith: "through faith... to all and on all who believe." It is faith, not works, that obtains God's righteousness. It is faith, not the law. It is faith, not human effort. It is faith that merely accepts what God has done for us in giving His Son to die for our sins. Just as we all have sinned and need God's righteousness, so also we all can now be justified.

Your Turn

2. Explain how a person can be "not guilty" before God, while imperfect in character or conduct.

_____

_____

_____

Again, by way of emphasis, the above verses say that we are justified "freely by His grace." As we have already seen, grace is defined as a free gift. So to say we are justified freely by His grace may seem repetitious, but this is for a reason.

Your Turn

3. What do you think is the reason for this repetition?

_____

_____

Romans says our salvation is *absolutely free!* Free to us, that is. But *God* paid a great price—His Son. That is why verse 24 calls it a "redemption" or a purchase. The amazing thing about salvation by grace is that we get so much absolutely free because God paid the highest price imaginable—the death of His only Son, Jesus Christ.

Some people erroneously speak of "cheap grace" or "costly grace." But grace is neither cheap nor costly. There is only one kind of grace—free grace. What we *can* say, however, is that *redemption* is costly because it cost God His own Son. Redemption was costly to God, that's why grace is free to us. To talk of cheap grace or costly grace strips grace of its essential meaning. Grace costs us absolutely nothing because by definition it is absolutely free.

If anything is clear about the explanation of salvation in Romans, it is that it is by grace. Since it is by grace, it can only be received by us through faith. It cannot be earned. If we could earn it or merit it in any way, we could boast.

But we cannot earn it, or it would not be by grace. That is why the writer of Romans asks,

Where is boasting then? It is excluded. By what law? Of works? No, but by the law of faith. Therefore we conclude that a man is justified by faith apart from the deeds of the law. (Romans 3:27-28)

If we could boast about earning our salvation (as many religious people do), we would glorify ourselves instead of God. But He has arranged our salvation in a way that only gives Him the glory He deserves as God. It is only through faith that we can be declared acceptable to God.

Your Turn

4. This imaginary scenario may help you understand why God will not allow us to earn our salvation. Let's say you are a judge who has a guilty friend in prison sentenced to die. You also have an only son. Because of your son's great love for this friend, your son volunteers to take your friend's place so he can be set free. The exchange takes place and your son is executed while your friend goes free. Later, you hear that this friend is telling everyone that he earned his freedom from prison through his good behavior. The most precious thing you had, your only son, died for your friend's freedom, but he has ignored what your son did and is bragging that he earned his freedom by his own effort! Write a few lines below that describe how your friend's claim would make you feel.

_____

_____

How might the same words describe how God must feel when someone boasts of earning or deserving salvation because of good works or commitments made to God while ignoring the gift of His one and only Son?

_____

_____

The concept of grace in salvation is so important that the writer of Romans goes to great length to illustrate it. He uses the popular Old Testament figure of Abraham as an example of someone saved through faith alone.
For what does the Scripture say? "Abraham believed God, and it was

accounted to him for righteousness." Now to him who works, the wages are not counted as grace, but as debt.

But to him who does not work, but believes on Him who justifies the ungodly, his faith is accounted for righteousness. (Romans 4:3-5)

 Your Turn

5. This passage is quoting the Old Testament book of Genesis 15:6. How is it used to show how Abraham obtained God's righteousness?

_____

_____

What did good works contribute to Abraham's salvation (and ours)?

_____

_____

If salvation by works was possible, salvation would be considered a debt owed to us by God. But in our salvation, God gives a gift; He does not pay a wage. Only if we do not work for it, but simply believe God for it, can we be declared righteous. Abraham was *not* declared righteous before God because he was circumcised or because he kept the law. Both circumcision and the law came after he was declared righteous (See Romans 4:9-25). This proves that his salvation, like ours, was through faith alone.

Romans goes on to show us that grace is a new realm in which to live. Grace places us in a new position before God.

Therefore, having been justified by faith, we have peace with God through our Lord Jesus Christ, through whom also we have access by faith into this grace in which we stand, and rejoice in hope of the glory of God. (Romans 5:1-2)

This new relationship with God brings us many other blessings. As you read the next verses from Romans 5:3-11, underline the main blessings that you find.

And not only that, but we also glory in tribulations, knowing that tribulation produces perseverance; and perseverance, character; and character, hope. Now hope does not disappoint, because the love of God has been poured out in our hearts by the Holy Spirit who was given to us.

For when we were still without strength, in due time Christ died for the ungodly. For scarcely for a righteous man will one die; yet perhaps for a good man someone would even dare to die. But God demonstrates His own love toward us, in that while we were still sinners, Christ died for us. Much more then, having now been justified by His blood, we shall be saved from wrath through Him. For if when we were enemies we were reconciled to God through the death of His Son, much more, having been reconciled, we shall be saved by His life. And not only that, but we also rejoice in God through our Lord Jesus Christ, through whom we have now received the reconciliation.

 Your Turn
6. Look back at Romans 5:1-11. Are there any of these blessings that you do not understand? Discuss these.

How wonderful is the grace of God! We receive everything for our salvation for nothing! A story illustrates this amazing truth:

A wealthy man lost his son in World War II. He grieved for many years. One day he was contacted by a man who said he served in the army with this son and he wanted to give the father something. When they finally met, the former soldier showed the father a pencil portrait of the son. It was not of the highest artistic quality, but a fair representation. The man told the father that he drew the portrait shortly before the son died trying to retrieve a fallen friend under gunfire. He wanted to give it to the father. The old man gratefully took it, and though he possessed many valuable pieces of art, he found his greatest pleasure in the simple drawing. Eventually the father died. In his will he stipulated that his art collection be auctioned off, including the sketch of his son. On the day of the auction, the son's portrait was offered first, but there were no bids. The audience protested that they should move on to the more valuable pieces of art. But the auctioneer explained that the deceased owner had stipulated in his will that the drawing of his son be auctioned first. Finally, an old man stood and said, "I knew the boy in the drawing. I will give $10 for it." "Sold!" cried the auctioneer. Then he added, "The auction is over." When the stunned audience demanded an explanation, the auctioneer explained, "The boy's father also stipulated in his will that whoever gets the picture of his son, will also get the rest of his art collection."

That's how it is when we receive the Son of God through faith. We get all the blessings listed in Romans 5:1-11 (and more!), and it doesn't cost us anything (not even $10!). It is by grace. Eternal life and all its blessings for *nothing!*

Living in the Family of Grace

---

continued on page 37

Please Explain...

Why are saved people told that they "shall be saved?"

You may think it odd that in Romans 5:9 the writer addresses those who have been justified and tells them they "shall be saved from wrath through Him [Christ]." Up to this point, we have been using the term "saved" and "salvation" to indicate initial salvation, which is also called justification. But the Bible also can refer to salvation in terms of God's comprehensive plan for us from beginning to end. That salvation is always from sin and its effects, but in different ways at different times, depending on the writer's focus. We should think of salvation as one event with three aspects:

In the past
- saved from the penalty of sin
- justification
- declared righteous

In the present
- saved from the power of sin
- sanctification
- becoming righteous

In the future
- saved from the presence of sin
- glorification
- made righteous

While justification refers to the legal declaration that we are acceptable to God, sanctification refers to the process of our becoming more like Jesus Christ in this life. Then glorification refers to the time when we will be made like Jesus Christ in all of His glory when we go to be with Him or when He comes for us. You see that Romans is moving forward toward a goal. It discusses the first aspect of salvation—justification—mostly in chapters 3-5.

Sin is the only thing that keeps us from enjoying these wonderful benefits of a new relationship with God. But Jesus Christ has paid the penalty of sin. The writer of Romans contrasts what Jesus Christ did with what Adam did with his first sin (called "offense" in this passage).

But the free gift is not like the offense. For if by the one man's offense many died, much more the grace of God and the gift by the grace of the one Man, Jesus Christ, abounded to many. (Romans 5:15)

Your Turn

7. How are Jesus Christ and Adam contrasted?

In contrasting Adam's sin and our condition under it, Romans declares that God's grace is sufficient to deal with our sin and death.

But where sin abounded, grace abounded much more, so that as sin reigned in death, even so grace might reign through righteousness to eternal life through Jesus Christ our Lord. (Romans 5:20b-21)

Though sin ruled us, God dethroned sin, paid its penalty, and declared us righteous by His grace. His grace was sufficient to forgive our sins, pay the penalty of death, and give us eternal life. God's grace is always greater than our sin. There is *no* sin that cannot be forgiven in Jesus Christ except persistent unbelief!

Points to Remember

— As sinners, we can be justified freely by grace through faith.

— Works that we do to earn eternal life are contrary to faith in God's grace.

— Our salvation by grace gives us a new position before God.

— In that position we have many other blessings of grace.

Please Explain...

Why are saved people told that they "shall be saved?"

continued from page 36

Then chapters 6-8 largely speak of our sanctification in this life, while the end of chapter 8 assures us of our future glorification. The verses above indicate that since we are now justified on the basis of Christ's death, we are in a position to be saved (delivered) from God's wrath and sin's effects in this life through the power of Christ's life in us.

Please Explain...

Is it fair to be condemned for Adam's sin?

In Genesis 2-3, the Bible explains how Adam, the first man, committed the first sin by disobeying God's command to not eat the forbidden fruit. Romans is saying that this one sin brought death and separation from God to the whole human race. Some might think this is unfair, because they were not there with Adam and did not commit the sin themselves. But there are three possible reasons why we are held accountable for Adam's sin. First, we actually were there! Every human being was present in Adam genetically and physically. As his descendants we have inherited Adam's sin and guilt just as one might inherit from his or her parents brown eyes or a serious disease like diabetes. Second, Adam was the representative head of the human race. As our representative, he led us into sin and its condemnation. It is a fact of life that those who lead us greatly affect our lives,

continued on page 38

Is it fair to be condemned for Adam's sin?

continued from page 37

sometimes negatively. A father falls asleep at the wheel and his whole family dies. A president declares war and the whole nation is offically at war, including women and children. Third, we sin. Can anyone really object that our condemnation is unfair when we have more than enough sin of our own to account for?

Finally, consider this: whoever concludes that our guilt is unfair and undeserved must also conclude that the death of the guiltless Son of God was also unfair and undeserved. But He died so that we could be pardoned from our guilt and have eternal life for nothing— absolutely free! But that is unfair and undeserved. We should thank God that grace is not fair—it's free!

Your Turn

8. Review the list of benefits of salvation in Romans 5:1-11. Explain which ones mean the most to you and why.

_____

_____

_____

_____

_____

_____

_____

_____

Take it to Heart
Memorize these verses:

Romans 3:24 *Being justified freely by His grace through the redemption that is in Christ Jesus.*

Romans 4:5 *But to him who does not work but believes on Him who justifies the ungodly, his faith is accounted for righteousness.*

The more we appreciate God's saving grace, the more we should want to live in a way that pleases Him. But now that we are no longer under the rule of sin, how should we live under the rule of grace? The next lesson will tell you how to live victoriously over sin.

Lesson 5: God's Grace and Our Sanctification, Part A: A New Identity

A Look Back
Explain justification and recite the two memory verses from the previous lesson.

A Look Ahead
You will learn how your new identity in Christ should affect your life.

Romans has explained about our sin, then our justification by grace through faith. Now it explains our sanctification. The word *sanctification* or *sanctify* is from the word *holy,* and means *to set apart,* or *to be made holy.* We are set apart or sanctified positionally at the moment of our justification, progressively in our daily lives, and ultimately when we go to be with the Lord. When used of the Christian life, sanctification usually means that we are progressively set apart unto God in our experience. Progressive sanctification is the process of having our *practice* as Christians line up with our *position* as Christians. Or since we have been adopted into God's family, we now begin to grow as His children to become like Him.

Your Turn
1. What is the only condition you saw for *justification* in the last lesson (on Romans 3:21—5:21)?

In contrast, can you list any of the Bible's commands and conditions you know of for *sanctification?*

Please Explain...

What's the difference between justification and progressive sanctification?

While justification and sanctification are necessarily related, they are also distinct in significance. We cannot be sanctified until we are justified, but the two truths should never be confused with each other. This chart will help you understand the important distinctions between justification and sanctification.

Justification
- We are declared righteous.
- A judicial declaration of our innocence
- Is free to us
- Our spiritual birth
- Happens to us in an instant
- Through faith in Jesus as Savior
- God's commitment to us
- Our position in God's family
- Determines our eternal destiny

Sanctification
- We become righteous.
- A practical experience of our growth
- Is costly to us
- Our spiritual growth
- Happens to us over a lifetime
- Through obedience to Jesus as Lord
- Our commitment to God
- Our practice as God's children
- Determines our eternal rewards

continued on page 40

Please Explain...

What's the difference between justification and progressive sanctification?

continued from page 39

The importance of these distinctions cannot be emphasized too much. The Bible speaks clearly about the distinctions between our positional justification and our practical sanctification. The condition for our justification is faith alone in Christ alone, but there are many conditions for sanctification. If we confuse the two, then we might wrongly conclude that the conditions for sanctification (such as: obedience, commitment, submission, good works) are conditions for justification. But since we know that justification is by grace through faith, the Bible's commands for obedience, commitment, submission, and good works are conditions only for our sanctification. If these were conditions for our justification, salvation would be by works instead of faith!

Please Explain...

What's the difference between Spirit baptism and water baptism?

Romans 6:3-4 speaks of a spiritual baptism which is different from water baptism. Every believer is baptized by the Holy Spirit the moment he or she believes in Jesus Christ as Savior (see 1 Corinthians 12:13). This refers to the action of the Spirit Who places the new believer into the invisible Body of Christ. That is why a believer can be described

continued on page 41

Now that justification has given us new life, how can we enjoy it? Growing in our new life with God requires that we understand our new position in grace. There is always the possibility of misunderstanding or under-appreciating the significance of God's grace. That is why the writer of Romans begins chapter 6 with a clarification. Since Romans 5:20 told us that God's grace abounds in proportion to our sins, someone could conclude incorrectly that sin would be a good course to follow because it brings a greater experience of God's grace. The writer anticipates this faulty reasoning:
What shall we say then? Shall we continue in sin that grace may abound? (Romans 6:1)

But the writer is repulsed by the idea, so he responds,
Certainly not! How shall we who died to sin live any longer in it? (Romans 6:2)

Then the writer explains why we should not live in sin. It involves our spiritual (not water) baptism (or immersion) by the Holy Spirit into the invisible body of Christ when we believed. Water baptism is only a visible picture of our invisible Spirit baptism.
Or do you not know that as many of us as were baptized into Christ Jesus were baptized into His death? Therefore we were buried with Him through baptism into death, that just as Christ was raised from the dead by the glory of the Father, even so we also should walk in newness of life. For if we have been united together in the likeness of His death, certainly we also shall be in the likeness of His resurrection. (Romans 6:3-5)

 Your Turn
2. **What did spiritual baptism do for us?**

As Christians, we are now in a special spiritual union with Jesus Christ. Because of our union with Christ, we have a new identity with God where He sees us in His Son. Since Jesus died to the rule of sin, in God's eyes so have we. Just as Jesus is raised to new life, in God's eyes so are we. Since Jesus cannot be ruled by sin, we are no longer slaves to sin like we were in our old selves. We have been freed from that old master!:

Knowing this, that our old man was crucified with Him, that the body of sin might be done away with, that we should no longer be slaves of sin. For he who has died has been freed from sin. Now if we died with Christ, we believe that we shall also live with Him, knowing that Christ, having been raised from the dead, dies no more. Death no longer has dominion over Him. For the death that He died, He died to sin once for all; but the life that He lives, He lives to God. (Romans 6:6-10)

Your Turn

3. According to these verses, why are we no longer slaves to our old master, sin?

_____

_____

_____

_____

The old master, sin, has no more power or authority over us. We are now under a new Master, the Lord Jesus Christ. But Christ died to sin and now lives for God. It is the same way for us. This truth addresses our position, not our experience. It is like a man who is a citizen of an oppressive country moving his citizenship to a free country. Though legally (in position) the former country can no longer control him, in reality (experience) the man can choose to live under the old oppressive rules.

The next verses tell us that to live consistently with our new status requires a calculated change in our thinking:

Likewise you also, reckon yourselves to be dead indeed to sin, but alive to God in Christ Jesus our Lord. Therefore do not let sin reign in your mortal body, that you should obey it in its lusts. And do not present your members as instruments of unrighteousness to sin, but present yourselves to God as being alive from the dead, and your members as instruments of righteousness to God. For sin shall not have dominion over you, for you are not under law but under grace. (Romans 6:11-14)

Please Explain...

What's the difference between Spirit baptism and water baptism?

continued from page 40

as "in Christ." This spiritual union with Jesus Christ gives us a new identity. Perhaps this chart will help you understand the difference between Spirit baptism and water baptism.

Spirit baptism
- Every believer receives it
- Essential to our eternal salvation
- Occurs at the moment of belief
- An invisible event
- An invisible inner reality
- Unites us with the invisible Body of Christ
- Unites us with Christ's death and resurrection

Water baptism
- Not every believer receives it
- Not essential to our eternal salvation
- May occur anytime after belief
- A visible event
- A visible outward testimony
- Unites us with the visible community of Christ
- Illustrates our union with Christ's death and resurrection

The more we "reckon" (which means to consider or consciously take to heart) our position as those free to serve God instead of as slaves to sin, the less we will serve sin and the more we will serve God with our lives. We must accept and live in this new identity. This perspective is essential for victory over the reality of sinful desires that remain in us.

Perhaps you've noticed that up to 6:11 in the book of Romans, we have not been commanded to do anything. This is the first command in the book. It is a command to seriously consider or calculate the significance of our position in and identity with Jesus Christ. Up to now the writer has devoted himself to explaining about our need, God's provision, and the blessing of our new relationship with God.

 Your Turn
4. Why do you think the writer would discuss the wonderful benefits of God's grace at such great length before he tells us anything that God wants us to do? Write a brief answer below.

_____

_____

_____

_____

_____

The blessings of grace should motivate us to live for God. It is hard to imagine any other response to Him. But since we are no longer under the law, but under grace, someone could conclude that we are free to do whatever we want. Certainly, we are free to choose to sin, but the writer anticipates the faulty reasoning behind such a choice and rejects it.

What then? Shall we sin because we are not under law but under grace? Certainly not! Do you not know that to whom you present yourselves slaves to obey, you are that one's slaves whom you obey, whether of sin leading to death, or of obedience leading to righteousness? (Romans 6:15-16)

If we obey our sinful desires, we become enslaved to them. Since we are slaves to God, we should submit ourselves to Him.

For just as you presented your members as slaves of uncleanness, and of lawlessness leading to more lawlessness, so now present your members as instruments of righteousness to God. (Romans 6:19b)

Living in the Family of Grace

We have a choice, and our choice has consequences. Will we serve sin or God? *For when you were slaves of sin, you were free in regard to righteousness. What fruit did you have then in the things of which you are now ashamed? For the end of those things is death. But now having been set free from sin, and having become slaves of God, you have your fruit to holiness, and the end, everlasting life. For the wages of sin is death, but the gift of God is eternal life in Christ Jesus our Lord.* (Romans 6:20-23)

Your Turn

5. How are the consequences for serving sin and serving God described?

_____

_____

_____

_____

"Death" describes the experience of becoming further separated from our fellowship (that is, our friendly relationship) with God, because we experience the deadening effects of sin and God's anger in our lives. But If we serve God, we become more righteous and holy as we enjoy the eternal life He has given us.

While slavery to other human beings is a repulsive idea, slavery to God is a good thing because God is good and always wants the best for us. If our slavery to God is good, then our only burden is not *doing* what God wants; rather, it is *not wanting to do* what God wants. Cooperating with God makes us want what He wants and is the only way to true peace and happiness. The alternative is to live in the experience of death.

Your Turn

6. Can you think of a time when you didn't obey God and therefore experienced the deadening effects of your sin in your fellowship with God? How did it affect you?

_____

_____

_____

As God's children, we are free from the obligations of the law, but that freedom should not be abused. We are not free to do what we want. Instead, we are free to do what *God* wants. True freedom is in doing God's will, because His will always has our benefit in view. When we voluntarily do what God wants, we avoid the negative consequences that sin would bring. So we are free, but free to serve God. A man named P. T. Forsyth said, "The first duty of every soul is to find not its freedom, but its master."

The greatest experience of God's eternal life both now and forever comes from serving God's will instead of our own. On the other hand, if a Christian lives selfishly in sin, he suffers a deadening separation from the enjoyment of God's life.

Points to Remember
— Sanctification refers to the process of growth as a child of God.

— The Spirit's baptism united us with Christ and gave us a new identity in Christ.

— Though we are free from sin's authority, sin remains in us.

— We must choose to serve God to grow in holiness and avoid the consequences of sin.

Your Turn
7. Explain how your new identity should make you think about yourself and how you should live.

_____

_____

_____

_____

_____

_____

_____

_____

Take it to Heart

Memorize these verses:

Romans 6:13 *And do not present your members as instruments of unrighteousness to sin, but present yourselves to God as being alive from the dead, and your members as instruments of righteousness to God.*

Romans 6:23 *For the wages of sin is death, but the gift of God is eternal life in Christ Jesus our Lord.*

You now see what it means to have a new identity, but in the next lesson you will see that along with that new identity comes a new power.

Lesson 6: God's Grace and Our Sanctification, Part B: A New Power

A Look Back

Explain what progressive sanctification is and recite the two memory verses from the previous lesson.

A Look Ahead

You will learn how the power of God's Spirit helps you live victoriously over sin.

A new identity means we are no longer under the old authority of sin, but it also means that we have a new power over sin. Our sanctification is not simply a matter of our own will power. Sanctification involves our cooperation and effort as we continually struggle with the sinful desires that remain in us. If anyone thinks the Christian life is a matter of self will or trying harder, then he should read of the writer's struggle with sin, which almost brought him to the point of despair. This is his experience when he tried to do it in his own strength:

For we know that the law is spiritual, but I am carnal, sold under sin. For what I am doing, I do not understand. For what I will to do, that I do not practice; but what I hate, that I do. If, then, I do what I will not to do, I agree with the law that it is good. But now, it is no longer I who do it, but sin that dwells in me. For I know that in me (that is, in my flesh) nothing good dwells; for to will is present with me, but how to perform what is good I do not find. For the good that I will to do, I do not do; but the evil I will not to do, that I practice. Now if I do what I will not to do, it is no longer I who do it, but sin that dwells in me. I find then a law, that evil is present with me, the one who wills to do good. For I delight in the law of God according to the inward man. But I see another law in my members, warring against the law of my mind, and bringing me into captivity to the law of sin which is in my members. O wretched man that I am! Who will deliver me from this body of death? (Romans 7:14-24)

Your Turn

1. What do you see as the source of this man's struggle?

_____

_____

_____

Why do you think he could not win this struggle?

_____

_____

_____

Though the writer knew what was right, when he relied on his own strength he still did what was wrong. Do you identify with his inner struggle to overcome sin by mere self effort? As long as we are in this present body, sinful urges will persist because though our sins are forgiven, our old sinful nature has left its influence. It is frustrating when we know what is right to do, but we fail to do it. Though sin no longer has the right to rule over us, it can sometimes exert itself in us as a powerful force. Just as a snake with its head cut off can twist and writhe for quite a while afterward, so the rule of death is destroyed, but its influence can still be felt in our bodies. So in our struggle with sin, how can we have the victory? If we can't do it on our own, what power can overcome our sinful urges so that we can obey God and do right? Happily, the writer has the answer for us:

I thank God—through Jesus Christ our Lord! So then, with the mind I myself serve the law of God, but with the flesh the law of sin. (Romans 7:25)

Your Turn

2. What is the answer to his problem?

_____

_____

To do the will of God and experience victory over sin, we must let Christ live His life in us through His Spirit who lives in us. This happens as we fix our minds on Him, because the mind controls the body. The power of the Holy Spirit controlling our minds will overcome the power of sin that wants to control our bodies.

Next, we will discover how Jesus gives this victory over sin. Chapter 8 of Romans gives the key to victorious Christian living.

What role does the Holy Spirit play in the Christian's life?

As you study Romans 8, you will see that the Holy Spirit plays a crucial role in every Christian's life. At the moment we believed in Christ as Savior, the Spirit gave us new birth (John 3:3), came to live in us (John 14:17), baptized us into the Body of Christ (1 Corinthians 12:13), and sealed us to guarantee our future with Christ (Ephesians 1:13-14).

As Christians, the Holy Spirit does many things for us.

- He comforts us (John 14:16).
- He teaches us (John 14:26).
- He guides us into truth (John 15:13).
- He gives us the power of Christ's life (Romans 8:11).
- He gives us victory over sin (Romans 8:13).
- He leads us to live a righteous life (Romans 8:14).
- He bears witness that we are God's children (Romans 8:16).
- He intercedes for us with God (Romans 8:26).
- He gives us spiritual gifts (1 Corinthians 12:11).
- He bears spiritual fruit in our lives (Galatians 5:22-23).
- He fills us with His power or character (Ephesians 5:18).

In short, the Holy Spirit is Christ's presence and power in us. He gives us every advantage of intimate fellowship with God. That fellowship can be interrupted if we grieve the Spirit with our sin (Ephesians 4:30) or quench the Spirit by suppressing His expression in others (1 Thessalonians 5:19).

There is therefore now no condemnation to those who are in Christ Jesus, who do not walk according to the flesh, but according to the Spirit. For the law of the Spirit of life in Christ Jesus has made me free from the law of sin and death. For what the law could not do in that it was weak through the flesh, God did by sending His own Son in the likeness of sinful flesh, on account of sin: He condemned sin in the flesh, that the righteous requirement of the law might be fulfilled in us who do not walk according to the flesh but according to the Spirit. For those who live according to the flesh set their minds on the things of the flesh, but those who live according to the Spirit, the things of the Spirit. For to be carnally minded is death, but to be spiritually minded is life and peace. (8:1-6)

Your Turn

3. How would you explain the key to victory over sin?

_____

_____

_____

Why do you think the mind is so important in our struggle with sin?

_____

_____

_____

Through Jesus Christ we are no longer condemned to a life of serving sin with its consequences. God overthrew the power of sin and fulfilled all the requirements of the law that we could not fulfill, because in our humanity we were too weak. In our new identity, we now also have the power of the Holy Spirit in us! To choose to go back and live under the power of sin is to set our mind "on the things of the flesh" or to have a sin-controlled mind. But to choose to focus on the Spirit's presence and power is to set our mind on "the things of the Spirit." Whatever becomes the focus of our mind changes our lives. We have a choice: We can live in the turmoil of deadness towards God, or we can live in the peace of God's dynamic and eternal life.

We can never please God when we live according to our sinful desires. The writer explains why:

Because the carnal mind is enmity against God; for it is not subject to the law of God, nor indeed can be. (Romans 8:7)

Your Turn

4. Why can't we please God when we live according to our sinful desires ("carnal mind")?

_____

_____

Since we are no longer under the rule of sin, but the Spirit who dwells in us, we should live according to the Spirit. His power frees us from the power of sin. His higher law overrules the lower one. For example, if you drop a nail it will fall to the ground because of the law of gravity. However, if you put the nail to a magnet, the nail will not fall because the law of magnetism supersedes the law of gravity. Likewise, a caterpillar is confined to the earth by the law of gravity until it becomes a butterfly and can fly by the law of aerodynamics. The Holy Spirit's power overrules sin's power so that we can live for God if we consciously acknowledge the Spirit's presence and His desires for us.

The writer goes on to remind us of our new position in Christ as he names some of the family privileges we can enjoy in that position:

So then, those who are in the flesh cannot please God. But you are not in the flesh but in the Spirit, if indeed the Spirit of God dwells in you. Now if anyone does not have the Spirit of Christ, he is not His. And if Christ is in you, the body is dead because of sin, but the Spirit is life because of righteousness. But if the Spirit of Him who raised Jesus from the dead dwells in you, He who raised Christ from the dead will also give life to your mortal bodies through His Spirit who dwells in you. (Romans 8:8-11)

Your Turn

5. What are the privileges we have because of our new position in Christ?

_____

_____

_____

Here the writer uses the phrase "in the flesh" to refer to our position when we were unsaved and under the rule of sin. But now in every one of God's children, the life of the risen Lord Jesus Christ is present to give us the same powerful resurrection life that Jesus displayed. This life comes to us through

His Spirit and has a present and future benefit. The Holy Spirit not only gives us victory over the deadening effects of sin in this life, but He also assures us of our future and final victory over all sin and eternal death through the resurrection of our body.

This privilege of being directed by God's Spirit into a life of righteousness is another privilege that only God's children can enjoy. It is a family privilege. The writer says,
For as many as are led by the Spirit of God, these are sons of God.
(Romans 8:14)

The Spirit of God within us also gives us a special intimate fellowship with God that is not based on fear, but on love.
For you did not receive the spirit of bondage again to fear, but you received the Spirit of adoption by whom we cry out, "Abba, Father." The Spirit Himself bears witness with our spirit that we are children of God.
(Romans 8:15-16)

The fellowship which we have with God as His children is so intimate we can even address him as "Papa." That is the meaning of the word "Abba." It is not a term of disrespect, but of intimacy. Isn't it wonderful to have full acceptance with our Heavenly Father so we do not have to fear Him, but can approach Him as our "Papa?"

Your Turn
6. What kind of things do you think should characterize a healthy fellowship between a human father and son?

_____

_____

_____

_____

What implications does this have for your fellowship with God as your Heavenly Father?

_____

_____

_____

_____

Contrast this kind of relationship with the enslaving fear that keeps us away from God. Under the old life, you may have sensed that you did not know God intimately as a Father. Perhaps you felt guilty and deserving of punishment because of your sin. Even when you tried to be good, you never knew when you were good enough to be acceptable to God. But now, you are accepted unconditionally because God adopted you. The fear is gone! God loves you as He loves His own Son! You are His forever! This is grace!

This full acceptance as children in God's family gives us another precious privilege which the writer describes:
and if children, then heirs—heirs of God and joint heirs with Christ, if indeed we suffer with Him, that we may also be glorified together.
(Romans 8:17)

As God's children, we are all heirs to eternal life. But those who endure suffering faithfully because of their identity with Christ, will also be "co-heirs with Christ." (This is clearer if you place the second comma after "God" instead of after "Christ," which is probably how this verse should be translated.) The reward for those who suffer is to be "glorified together" with Jesus. This refers to the reward of sharing in Christ's glorious rule in His coming kingdom. So while all who know Jesus as Savior will *enter* the kingdom, those who are faithful in suffering for Him will be *rewarded* in the kingdom.

The writer then offers this encouragement for those who suffer:
For I consider that the sufferings of this present time are not worthy to be compared with the glory which shall be revealed in us. (Romans 8:18)

Your Turn

7. What is the encouragement in this verse?

_____

_____

_____

As a child of God, you should have an eternal perspective on life. This life will pass, and God's glory in His kingdom will follow. The greatness of His glory that we will share in His kingdom will make our present sufferings seem less significant.

Yet another privilege of adoption into God's family is that His Spirit helps us to pray when we are suffering:
Likewise the Spirit also helps in our weaknesses. For we do not know what we should pray for as we ought, but the Spirit Himself makes intercession

for us with groanings which cannot be uttered. Now He who searches the hearts knows what the mind of the Spirit is, because He makes intercession for the saints according to the will of God. (Romans 8:26-27)

We can be sure that God's Spirit will pray for us according to God's will because the Spirit knows God's mind. There are times in the life of a Christian when we feel so weak, overwhelmed, or worried that we cannot even think to pray. Sometimes we just do not know exactly what is the best way to pray in a difficult situation. At these times we have the promise that God's Spirit will pray for us in exactly the right way.

You see that growing in the Christian life takes cooperation with God. It is not a matter of willpower, but Spirit-power. Aren't you thankful that God has given us His Spirit to empower us to live for Him?

 Points to Remember
— Our sinful desires conflict with our desire to please God.

— Our own willpower is not enough to conquer our sinful desires.

— To have victory over sin, we must focus our mind on His Spirit's presence and power.

— The Holy Spirit blesses us with life-giving power and intimacy with God our Father.

 Your Turn
8. To review, look for statements in Romans 6, 7, and 8 that compare or contrast the fleshly-minded Christian with the spiritually-minded Christian and fill in this chart.

The fleshly-minded Christian	The spiritually-minded Christian

Take It to Heart
Memorize these verses:

Romans 8:1 *There is therefore now no condemnation to those who are in Christ Jesus, who do not walk according to the flesh, but according to the Spirit.*

Romans 8:15 *For you did not receive the spirit of bondage again to fear, but you received the Spirit of adoption by whom we cry out, "Abba, Father."*

You are now ready to learn one of the most important privileges you are given as a child of God. You will find out what that is when you continue to the next lesson.

Lesson 7: God's Grace and Our Security

A Look Back
Explain how we can have victory over sin and recite the two memory verses from the previous lesson.

_____

_____

_____

A Look Ahead
In this lesson we will see that our future with Christ is secure.

This last section of Romans 8 is one of the most beautiful and important passages in the New Testament. It is a wonderful assurance of our future with Christ. It is a view of grace from the mountain top!

We have seen from Romans that we have many privileges as God's children. We have so much on our side, no wonder we can trust God to make things work out for us! This comforting assurance is given in the next verse.
And we know that all things work together for good to those who love God, to those who are called according to His purpose. (Romans 8:28)

When we are serving God according to His purpose, God will take every circumstance of our lives, good or bad, and use them for our eternal good. He will not let anything that happens to us stand in the way of accomplishing His eternal purpose for us. That purpose is explained in this way:
For whom He foreknew, He also predestined to be conformed to the image of His Son, that He might be the firstborn among many brethren. Moreover whom He predestined, these He also called; whom He called, these He also justified; and whom He justified, these He also glorified. (Romans 8:29-30)

God's eternal purpose for us as Christians began before time when He decided to make us His children. That is the significance of "He foreknew" and "He predestined." His plan was to make us like Jesus Christ.

Your Turn
1. What is the purpose or goal for every believer according to the passage above?

_____

_____

To make us like Jesus Christ, God uses an unbreakable sequence of experiences. Notice the progression in the last verse:

— All those who God predestined to be like Jesus are the same ones He called to salvation with the invitation of the gospel.

— All those who God called through the gospel are the same ones He justified.

— All those who God justified are the same ones He will glorify.

Your Turn

2. What does this unbreakable sequence imply about your future with Jesus Christ?

_____

_____

_____

Did you find any room in verses 29-30 for you or any other Christian to fall through the cracks? These events are linked like an unbreakable chain; your future glorification does not depend on your efforts or performance as God's child, but on God's eternal purpose. He purposed to accept you unconditionally as His child and bring you to be with Him forever. You can never be ejected from this process because it does not ultimately depend on you, but on the unfailing grace and power of God. (Note that progressive sanctification is not in the chain because it depends on our cooperation with God.) These critical verses give us the assurance that as God's children, we will never be expelled from His family. Every single one of us will be glorified with Christ in eternity just as God intended. It is grace from start to finish!

This is so crucial that we should not miss the implication: *No Christian can lose his or her eternal salvation!* Eternal life is a never-ending experience of God's life. It is never-ending, *not* temporary. Since we are saved by grace, we are kept saved by grace. God does not kick His children out of His family. Our acceptance in His family is based on His unconditional love and grace. Just as there is nothing we can do to earn a place in His family, so there is nothing we can do to lose it. For example, a plane ticket is an agreement to get you to your destination. There will be no mid-air examination of your life to see if you are worthy. Your fare has been paid in full and covers the whole trip from beginning to end. So it is with your salvation.

Please Explain...

Why do some Christians believe that they can lose their salvation?

Anyone who believes salvation can be lost does not fully understand God's magnificent grace. If salvation by grace means that it is a free gift that we do nothing to earn, then we certainly can do nothing to keep it. It is inconsistent to say that we are saved by grace but kept saved by faithful performance as Christians. In that system, salvation is really by works, or what one does or does not do. Besides this, it raises the question that no one can answer:

continued on page 56

continued from page 55

Your Turn
3. Someone might say that this security of salvation might cause Christians to sin. How would you respond?

_____

_____

_____

_____

_____

_____

The certainty of our salvation and the assurance that it can never be lost is amplified by the ending of the chapter. As if our secure salvation is too good to believe, the writer asks,
What then shall we say to these things? (Romans 8:31a)

It is as if the privileges the writer has mentioned are so incredibly awesome that they demand a response or conclusion of some kind. This conclusion is given in a series of four questions. In them the writer assures us that our relationship to God is eternally secure. Let's look at these questions one at a time.
If God is for us, who can be against us? (Romans 8:31b)

The first question asks who can undo God's favor towards us. If God is on our side working all things together for our eternal good, who can prevail against us? The answer of course is absolutely no one! But the writer answers this question with another question.
He who did not spare His own Son, but offered Him up for us all, how shall He not with Him also freely give us all things? (Romans 8:32)

Your Turn
4. What do you think this verse is saying?

_____

_____

_____

_____

God is so much on our side that He gave His own Son for us. If He gave us that great gift, will He not give us all the rest of His blessings? Since the gift of His Son obtained our initial salvation (justification), will God not finish our eternal salvation (glorification)? If He would not, then God would have wasted the gift of His Son on us! Notice again the word "freely." When we have the Son as a free gift, we have everything else just as freely. It is a package deal. Just as we do not pay for justification by the Son, neither can we pay for our glorification which follows. They are free according to the riches of God's grace! For example, if you wanted to honor your parents on their wedding anniversary with a free trip to London, you would certainly pay for their transportation there. But wouldn't you also pay for their hotel, meals, and other needs if you were able? Of course you would. God is more than able to give us every *good* thing since He has already given us the *best* thing—His Son!

Now the second question is asked and answered:
Who shall bring a charge against God's elect? It is God who justifies. (Romans 8:33)

Again, the implied answer is *absolutely no one!* This question assumes a courtroom scene where God is Judge and we are defendants. Is there anyone anywhere who can accuse us of anything that would jeopardize our standing with God? The answer of course is *no—no one, nothing.* God will not reverse His verdict. Here we are called "God's elect" (chosen ones) to remind us that God chose us knowing full well the charges against us and our guilt. He chose us anyway because He knew that we would be fully acquitted (declared "not guilty") of all charges.

Your Turn
5. On what basis could God acquit us of all our sins?

_____

_____

_____

The third question similarly has the courtroom in view:
Who is he who condemns? It is Christ who died, and furthermore is also risen, who is even at the right hand of God, who also makes intercession for us. (Romans 8:34)

Just as no one can charge us with any sin, neither can anyone condemn us for any sin. Notice the four parts of the answer. (1) Jesus was condemned for us when He died on the cross bearing our sins. Not only that, but the writer reminds us that (2) He also rose from the dead to show that God had accepted His sacrifice. (3) Now He is seated at the right hand of God where

In spite of these great assurances you have just read about, it is true that some Christians are plagued with doubts about their eternal salvation. Perhaps you have struggled with this yourself. Reasons for doubt vary:

• Some were perhaps never saved in the first place by accepting God's promise as true for themselves.

• Some may wonder if they have believed enough or in the "right" way.

• Some may have been influenced by the incorrect teaching that Christians can lose their salvation.

• Some may have trouble accepting God's unconditional acceptance because of rejection in past relationships.

• Some may have a personality that is introspective or more oriented towards feelings than facts.

• Some may have experienced a severe trial that made them question whether God really loves them.

• Some may be practicing a sinful lifestyle and have lost their feelings of joy and assurance of God's love.

• Some may simply be uninformed of the great truths of Romans 8 and other Bible passages.

Whatever the reason, no one needs to live with doubt about their salvation. To know for sure that you

continued on page 59

(4) He intercedes for us. The idea of interceding also echoes from the courtroom. It is a word that suggests a defense advocate who defends someone against charges. Jesus is our defense attorney and he has the ear of the Judge! With Jesus to defend us, there is nothing to condemn us. Jesus never loses a case!

The fourth and last question dramatically draws the chapter to a close. *Who shall separate us from the love of Christ?* (Romans 8:35a)

The writer wants to be sure that we understand the answer to this question, so he uses lofty language:

> *Shall tribulation, or distress, or persecution, or famine, or nakedness, or peril, or sword?*
> *As it is written:*
> *"For Your sake we are killed all day long;*
> *We are accounted as sheep for the slaughter."*

Yet in all these things we are more than conquerors through Him who loved us. For I am persuaded that neither death nor life, nor angels nor principalities nor powers, nor things present nor things to come, nor height nor depth, nor any other created thing, shall be able to separate us from the love of God which is in Christ Jesus our Lord. (Romans 8:35b-39)

Your Turn
6. What is the main point the writer is trying to communicate with such expressive words?

_____

_____

_____

_____

We have climbed to the mountain top of grace. Now what do we see? We see there is no one and nothing in all of creation that can come between us believers and the love of God. Absolutely nothing. God's love for His children cannot be revoked or nullified. Isn't this the most precious of assurances? You do not have to doubt for a moment that God loves you and always will love you. He loves you no matter what others may say or do to you. He loves you no matter what happens to you or what spiritual forces come against you. He loves you in spite of your feelings about yourself. We are more than victorious!

Child of God, you are so precious to your Heavenly Father that He will always love you. Such is the depth of His love for you. This is only possible because of God's infinite grace. If your salvation now and in the future depended on your performance in any way, you would not have these assurances of God's eternal love and acceptance. But because He saved you by His grace and brings His purpose for you to completion by His grace, you can know beyond all doubt that you are His child forever. Amen!

Your Turn

7. Have you ever doubted your salvation? If so, what was your thinking or the reason behind your confusion?

_____

_____

_____

Points to Remember

— God wants us to know for certain that we have eternal life.

— God will finish His purpose for every one of His children.

— Nothing can thwart God's purpose for us or come between us and His eternal love.

— Therefore, we can be sure we are securely saved.

Your Turn

8. Be sure to settle any doubts you have about your salvation right now before you continue any further in this study guide. Thank God that His promise of eternal life is true—true for you! Sign here as an expression of your assurance that is based on God's promise.

_____

Now write out a plan to follow if you ever begin to doubt in the future.

_____

_____

_____

Please Explain...

Why do some Christians have doubts about their salvation?

continued from page 58

are saved is the birthright of every Christian. It is not proud or presumptuous to believe you are saved, because it is merely trusting in God's many promises that whoever believes on His Son has eternal life at the very moment he or she believes. Our salvation is based on the facts of Christ's death and resurrection, not our feelings or our performance. We should not look inward to our feelings, because feelings change. Since these facts about Christ are objective, we can know we are saved eternally.

If Christians do not have this assurance, doubt and insecurity will hinder their spiritual growth and joyful service as children of God. Imagine the insecurity in a child who doubts whether he belongs to his family! If you struggle with doubts about your salvation, go back and read the four questions asked and answered in Roman 8:31-39. Will you not believe these are for you?

Take It to Heart

Memorize these verses:

Romans 8:28 *And we know that all things work together for good to those who love God, to those who are the called according to His purpose.*

Romans 8:38-39 *For I am persuaded that neither death nor life, nor angels nor principalities nor powers, nor things present nor things to come, nor height nor depth, nor any other created thing shall be able to separate us from the love of God which is in Christ Jesus our Lord!*

After learning these amazing truths about your secure standing with God, you might think that He could not bless you any more than He has. But there is more! You are part of God's eternal plan for the world. The next lesson introduces you to this plan.

Lesson 8: God's Grace and Our Selection

A Look Back

Explain how we can know for sure that we have eternal life and recite the two memory verses from the previous lesson.

_____

_____

_____

A Look Ahead

This lesson will help you see the big picture of how your salvation makes you a significant part of God's overall plan for the world.

We who believe in Jesus Christ have been saved by grace. Each of us has a glorious future with Him. By His grace, He has selected us as a part of His bigger plan for the rest of the world.

The writer of Romans has taken great effort to help us understand the wonderful grace of God in our salvation, sanctification, and glorification; in other words, from the beginning to the end of our salvation. The writer now explains in chapters 9-11 how God's grace is behind His plan for all people, both the Jews and the non-Jews (called Gentiles). By His sovereign will (which means He is free to do as He pleases) He selected Israel to be His people. But when they rejected His provision for righteousness, He sovereignly turned His blessings of grace on the Gentiles.

Chapters 9-11 may be the most difficult section to understand in the book of Romans. But when understood, they should inspire the deepest humility, worship, and service. God is sovereignly at work to accomplish His purposes in human history. We can actually call history _His story_, because it reveals God working to bring His offer of salvation to all the people of the world.

In chapters 1-8 of Romans, you saw how God's grace brought salvation to all who believed. You saw how wonderful the grace that saved you was. Now you will see how that same grace has made you part of God's bigger plan for the world. He has chosen you to be a part of His eternal purpose for the world! The key to understanding God's sovereign plan for the world is to understand what He is doing with the nation of Israel, the homeland of the Jewish people. The Jewish people had been chosen by God long ago to be the means by which He would bless the whole world. This was to be done through Jesus as their Messiah and King, but when He appeared, the nation rejected Him.

Why are the Jews called God's chosen people?

The Jews are called God's chosen people because He selected them from among all nations for a special blessing and made special promises to them called covenants. The initial selection occurred when God chose Abraham and promised him a land, a nation of descendants, and a special descendant, Jesus Christ, who would be a blessing to the whole world (Genesis 12). In Romans 9:4-5 you will find the special blessings God gave to the Jews:

- "the adoption" refers to His selection of and establishing of Israel as His people.

- "the glory" refers to God's special presence with Israel in their tabernacle and temple.

- "the covenants" refers to God's special promises to bless and keep Israel as His people forever.

- "the giving of the law" refers to the laws God gave to Israel through Moses.

- "the service of God" refers to the unique privilege Israel had to facilitate worship of God through the priestly service and sacrifices.

- "the promises" includes all the promises to bless the nation.

- "of whom are the fathers" refers to Jews as Abraham's descendants who also were promised the same blessings as Abraham.

- "from whom...Christ came" refers to the fact that Jesus, the Messiah, was a Jew.

Unfortunately, though Jesus belonged to the Jews, the Jews didn't belong to Jesus because

continued on page 63

The author of Romans, the Apostle Paul, was a Jew, but he was grieved that his people had rejected Jesus Christ as their Savior (or Messiah). He was so grieved, he said he was willing to be separated from Christ if it meant that Israel would come to accept Christ:

... I have great sorrow and continual grief in my heart. For I could wish that I myself were accursed from Christ for my brethren, my countrymen according to the flesh. (Romans 9:2-3)

Your Turn

1. The history of Israel shows that they did not deserve God's blessings. What does the fact that God chose them anyway teach us about God?

_____

_____

_____

_____

The fact that the nation of Israel had rejected Jesus as her Messiah and Savior did not mean that some individual Jews could not believe in Him. Romans 9:8 makes it clear that it is more than physical descent (race) that makes one a true Jew, or a child of God, who receives the promised blessings:
That is, those who are the children of the flesh, these are not the children of God; but the children of the promise are counted as the seed.

With this declaration, we see that anyone can receive God's blessings of salvation through the promised Messiah, if they only believe in Him.

Because the nation of Israel rejected the Messiah Jesus, God rejected Israel. That is, He temporarily turned His favor from them. It is His sovereign and free right to do so. As God first declared to Moses,
"... I will have mercy on whomever I will have mercy, and I will have compassion on whomever I will have compassion." (Romans 9:15)

But the rejection of Israel meant that God would now turn His favor on the Gentiles and offer them the same gift of righteousness through Jesus Christ. The writer of Romans points out that this was predicted in the Old Testament through the prophet Hosea:
> *As He also says in Hosea:*
> > *"I will call them My People, who are not My people,*
> > *And her beloved, who was not beloved."*
> > *"And it shall come to pass in the place where it was said to them,*

'You are not My people,'
There they shall be called 'sons of the living God.'" (Romans 9:25-26)

Your Turn
2. Whether you are a Jew or a Gentile by birth, how does God's sovereign choice to turn His favor to the Gentiles make you feel?

_____

_____

_____

_____

There is a great difference between the response of the Jews and the response of the Gentiles to God's offer of righteousness and salvation, as seen in these verses:

What shall we say then? That Gentiles, who did not pursue righteousness, have attained to righteousness, even the righteousness of faith; but Israel, pursuing the law of righteousness, has not attained to the law of righteousness. Why? Because they did not seek it by faith... (Romans 9:30-31a)

Your Turn
3. Why did the Gentiles receive God's righteousness while the Jews did not?

_____

_____

_____

God's righteousness was always near and available to the Jews, if they had only accepted it by accepting Jesus as their Messiah.

But what does it say? "The word is near you, in your mouth and in your heart" (that is, the word of faith which we preach): that if you confess with your mouth the Lord Jesus and believe in your heart that God has raised Him from the dead, you will be saved. For with the heart one believes unto righteousness, and with the mouth confession is made unto salvation." (Romans 10:8-10)

Please Explain...

Why are the Jews called God's chosen people?
continued from page 62

they rejected Him. This had consequences for the whole world. The fact that God chose the Jews to be His special people was not an end in itself. He purposed to use them to bless all the other people of the world (Gentiles) with the salvation that would come through the Jewish Messiah. But in rejecting Jesus as their Messiah, the Jews could not pass God's blessing of salvation on to the Gentiles. However, God used their failure to accomplish His purposes anyway. Still, God has a plan for the Jewish nation of Israel. That's what Romans 9-11 is about.

What does it mean to confess with your mouth?

Unfortunately, some people want to make *confess* mean that one must verbalize his or her faith in Christ, make a public profession, or demonstrate their faith through their conduct in life in order to be eternally saved. But you can easily see how this makes salvation dependent on something other than faith alone. Romans has been clear throughout, and especially in this section, that salvation is through faith alone in Christ alone (see Romans 10:4, 6, 11, 14, 17).

One interpretation of these verses that does not contradict salvation by grace through faith notes that the word *confess* literally means *to say the same thing as,* or in other words, *to agree.* Here it would simply mean that to receive God's righteousness, the Jews only needed to agree or admit the truth anticipated by their Old Testament which promised that the Messiah would come as God in the flesh to pay the penalty for sin and that He would be raised from the dead. This was a familiar teaching in Old Testament passages like Isaiah 53. For a Jew to admit that Jesus is Lord is to admit that Jesus is God, which is an admission that He is indeed the Messiah. So confess would be another way of saying that they must believe.

Another interpretation consistent with salvation by grace through faith understands the salvation of this passage as deliverance for the Jews from some danger. If they believe in Jesus Christ as their Messiah and subsequently confess or call out to God for help, they will be delivered either from their enemies or from

continued on page 65

Since Romans teaches that God has turned from working with Israel to working with Gentiles, it raises two questions. First, is God totally finished working with the Jewish people? And second, what will happen to Israel in the future?

The first question is asked and answered in Romans 11:1:
I say, then, has God cast away His people? Certainly not! For I also am an Israelite, of the seed of Abraham, of the tribe of Benjamin.

 Your Turn
4. What is the writer's (the Apostle Paul) proof that God is not finished with the Jewish people?

_____

_____

_____

_____

God has not totally ceased working with the Jewish people. Although the nation has not believed in Jesus like Paul has, God still saves individual Jews in spite of the national rejection. This is, as always, by God's grace:
Even so then, at this present time there is a remnant according to the election of grace. And if by grace, then it is no longer of works; otherwise grace is no longer grace. But if it is of works, it is no longer grace; otherwise work is no longer work. (Romans 11:5-6)

That God chooses to save some Jews is a work of His grace. Since their salvation rests in His sovereign selection, it has to be by grace; it cannot be by works. As the passage above points out, grace and works are mutually exclusive.

Your Turn
5. How would you try to explain our sovereign election with our responsibility to believe?

_____

_____

_____

_____

A second question is asked and answered in Romans 11:11a:
I say then, have they stumbled that they should fall? Certainly not! But through their fall, to provoke them to jealousy, salvation has come to the Gentiles.

In other words, though Israel has rejected Jesus as their Messiah and God has rejected Israel, it is not a final rejection. It is temporary and with a purpose—so that salvation could come to the Gentiles and thus make the Jews jealous. So now Gentiles are given the opportunity to come to faith in Jesus Christ and enjoy the promises first given to the Jews. Romans 11:16-24 illustrates this truth using an olive tree. Israel is the tree rooted in God's covenant promises, but Gentiles are like a branch grafted in to enjoy those same promises.

But this situation is not permanent. Romans explains how God will finish with the Gentiles and turn His favor back to the Jews.
For I do not desire, brethren, that you should be ignorant of this mystery, lest you should be wise in your own opinion, that blindness in part has happened to Israel until the fullness of the Gentiles has come in. And so all Israel will be saved …(Romans 11:25-26a)

Please Explain...

What does it mean to confess with your mouth?

continued from page 64

sin and its consequence of God's wrath (see 1:18). In 5:9-10 the writer said that those who have been justified (in the past) "shall be saved from wrath" (in the future) through Christ. In 10:14 confession seems to be subsequent to and distinct from believing. So in this view, confess would be an appeal to God by believers for help in trouble.

Both of the above interpretations can apply to Gentiles also, as indicated by verses 12-13. Both of these two interpretations show that confess is not a second condition for salvation in addition to faith.

Your Turn

6. According to these verses, what is God's ultimate future for Israel?

_____

_____

_____

_____

God's turning to the Gentiles is called a "mystery" (divine secret) because this period of Gentile salvation was not anticipated before the end of history. It began in the first century with the initial spread of the gospel of Jesus Christ and continues today. We call this era the Church Age. God's sovereign selection of Gentiles should cause them to be humble, not arrogant and proud. Besides, when God is finished working with the Gentiles, He will turn back to Israel to save them. Elsewhere the Bible tells us that this happens when Jesus Christ comes to set up His kingdom in the future.

Please Explain...

If God chooses who will be saved, why do we have to believe?

The idea of God's election, or choosing, of those who will be saved is controversial and not always easy to understand. Some find it difficult to reconcile this with the truth that our own faith is the necessary condition of salvation. But both are true and both are taught in the Bible! Election looks at salvation from God's sovereign perspective while faith looks at salvation from the perspective of human responsibility. God is able to make both sides of salvation work together in a way that is fair to all, but perhaps not easily explainable. No one will be saved who is not chosen and who does not also believe.

This causes some to ask, "If God chooses some to be saved and not others, is this fair to those who are not chosen?" Yes, because God is sovereign (free) to do as He wills. He says "I will show mercy to whomever I show mercy" (see Romans 9:15). Furthermore, He is fair because all are sinners undeserving of His grace. If He chooses to save some sinners, He is giving guilty sinners what they do not deserve. It must also be remembered that all are given the same opportunity to respond to God's truth and the gospel.

Another question sometimes asked is "How can I know if I am one of those who have been chosen for salvation, one of the elect?" We cannot know God's sovereign will. But looking at what we can know from the perspective of human responsibility, it is simply an issue of whether you believe in Jesus Christ as your Savior or not. If you have

continued on page 67

Ultimately, in God's sovereign plan, even His rejection of Israel is an opportunity for a greater display of His grace because salvation will come to both Jew and Gentile: *For God has committed them all to disobedience, that He might have mercy on all. (Romans 11:32)*

We have covered a lot of material in Romans 9-11. Perhaps it would be good to use a chart to summarize these truths historically.

Romans 9:1-29	Romans 9:30-10:21	Romans 11
Israel's past	Israel's present	Israel's future
Israel is given the promises	Israel rejects the promises; God rejects Israel, turns to Gentiles	God restores Israel
Old Testament Era	New Testament Era, or Church Age	Kingdom Era

Whether you are a Jew or a Gentile, if you have believed in Jesus Christ as your Savior, you have a glorious destiny as part of God's plan for the world. His grace not only covers your sin, it brings eternal salvation to all the people of the world in anticipation of Christ's coming kingdom.

Look at how this truth affected the writer of Romans. After discussing God's sovereign plan and purpose for the world, His gracious selection of Jews and Gentiles, and His promise to bring both into His kingdom, the writer of Romans breaks out into words of praise and worship.
Oh, the depth of the riches both of the wisdom and knowledge of God! How unsearchable are His judgments and His ways past finding out!
(Romans 11:33)

You may not understand why God has selected you to be a part of His universal plan. But you know that it is by His grace and by His sovereign will. This truth should overwhelm you with emotions similar to the writer's above.

 Points to Remember
— You are part of God's eternal purpose for the world.

— God has temporarily rejected Israel and turned to the Gentiles with His salvation.

— The salvation of Gentiles and the future restoration of Israel displays God's wonderful grace.

— We should worship God, because in His grace He has made us part of His eternal purpose.

Your turn

7. Now use your own words to express how you feel when you think that God has chosen you, given you all the promises of salvation, and made you part of His eternal and wise plan to bring salvation to all who believe.

_____

_____

_____

_____

_____

_____

Please Explain...

If God chooses who will be saved, why do we have to believe?

continued from page 66

believed in Him you have eternal life and are one of God's chosen. The fact of God's election never cancels the responsibility to believe.

Though we may not understand everything, the fact that our salvation rests ultimately in God's sovereign selection magnifies His grace.

Take it to Heart
Memorize these verses:

Romans 10:9-10 *That if you confess with your mouth the Lord Jesus and believe in your heart that God has raised Him from the dead, you will be saved. For with the heart one believes unto righteousness, and with the mouth confession is made unto salvation.*

Romans 11:6 *And if by grace, then it is no longer of works; otherwise grace is no longer grace. But if it is of works, it is no longer grace; otherwise work is no longer work!*

Now that you have been given the full scope of God's grace, you should not only feel emotions of gratitude and worship, you should want to express this attitude through all of your life. The next lesson tells us how we can respond to the grace of God.

Lesson 9: God's Grace and Our Service

A Look Back
Explain how you are part of God's plan for the world and recite the two memory verses from the previous lesson.

_____

_____

_____

A Look Ahead
This lesson will challenge you to respond to all that God has done for you.

Romans 9-11 showed how God has saved you to make you a part of His eternal plan for the world. Now we answer the question, *so what?*

Beginning in chapter 12, Romans discusses how we should respond to God's grace. What is an appropriate response to God for all that He has done for us? How should we live in the light of His assurances that we are His privileged children forever? How can we live so as to thank God for the many blessings that come to us through His Son?

Your Turn
1. Think of the nicest thing anyone has ever done for you. How did it make you feel? How did it make you want to act towards this person?

_____

_____

_____

In Romans 12 the writer begins a section that shows how a Christian should respond to God's grace. He tells us that we respond by serving Him with our lives.

I beseech you therefore, brethren, by the mercies of God, that you present your bodies a living sacrifice, holy, acceptable to God, which is your reasonable service. And do not be conformed to this world, but be transformed by the renewing of your mind, that you may prove what is that good and acceptable and perfect will of God. (Romans 12:1-2)

The writer appeals to us in view of all that he has told us so far. Because we have this immense privilege, "the mercies of God," in our salvation and sanctification, we should present ourselves to God as a sacrifice that He can use. We are a "living sacrifice" because we have the life-giving presence of the Holy Spirit in us. Here the writer uses a picture from the Old Testament when animals were sacrificed to God under the law. But there is a major difference. While under the law living animals were put to death, under grace we put to death our old selves and are made alive by the Spirit. Old Testaments sacrifices died and were used only once, but as living sacrifices we can continue to serve God. This pleases God and is our "reasonable service," or the only reasonable response to God's grace.

Your Turn

2. Why do you think spiritual transformation begins with the mind?

_____

_____

_____

_____

As living sacrifices, our mental processes should also be put to death, so that we can begin to think in a new way. The world system exerts great pressure to influence us to conform to its philosophies, values, morals, and thinking. To be useful to God, we cannot be shaped by the values and philosophies common to this age, but our thinking must change. It must be reshaped to value what God values.

The writer now names specific ways we Christians can live as sacrifices. The list is long, going from chapter 12:3 through chapter 15:13. Here is an example of some of the actions he names for us from chapter 12:3-21: _For I say, through the grace given to me, to everyone who is among you, not to think of himself more highly than he ought to think, but to think soberly, as God has dealt to each one a measure of faith. For as we have many members in one body, but all the members do not have the same function, so we, being many, are one body in Christ, and individually members of one another. Having then gifts differing according to the grace that is given to us, let us use them: if prophecy, let us prophesy in proportion to our faith; or ministry, let us use it in our ministering; he who teaches, in teaching; he who exhorts, in exhortation; he who gives, with liberality; he who leads, with diligence; he who shows mercy, with cheerfulness. Let love be without hypocrisy. Abhor what is evil. Cling to what is good. Be kindly affectionate to one another with brotherly love, in honor giving preference_

Please Explain...

How can our minds be renewed?

Though the writer tells us to "be transformed by the renewing of your mind," he does not tell us how. When he speaks of a renewed mind, he means that we should cultivate a spiritual mind that is sensitive to God's will for us. We need a conscious inner desire to please God. But how do we know how to please God? We know what God wants us to do from His Word, the Bible. Elsewhere, the Bible says we should feed on it as a baby feeds on his milk (1 Peter 2:2). It is the Holy Spirit's job to take the Word of God and apply it to our lives so that it shapes our attitudes and actions. You can see why it is important to regularly study and meditate on the Bible. As the truths of God's Word permeate us, the Holy Spirit changes us by renewing our minds.

to one another; not lagging in diligence, fervent in spirit, serving the Lord; rejoicing in hope, patient in tribulation, continuing steadfastly in prayer; distributing to the needs of the saints, given to hospitality. Bless those who persecute you; bless and do not curse. Rejoice with those who rejoice, and weep with those who weep. Be of the same mind toward one another. Do not set your mind on high things, but associate with the humble. Do not be wise in your own opinion. Repay no one evil for evil. Have regard for good things in the sight of all men. If it is possible, as much as depends on you, live peaceably with all men. Beloved, do not avenge yourselves, but rather give place to wrath; for it is written, "Vengeance is mine, I will repay," says the Lord. Therefore

> *"If your enemy is hungry, feed him;*
> *If he is thirsty, give him a drink;*
> *For in so doing you will heap coals of fire on his head."*
> *Do not be overcome by evil, but overcome evil with good.*

Your Turn

3. According to the beginning of this passage, what is the attitude that should govern our actions?

_____

_____

_____

List the three actions in this passage that challenge you the most.

1. _____

2. _____

3. _____

You can see that many kinds of actions are covered. These include service to God, service to others, attitudes, use of our gifts, and the proper response to someone who hurts you. That is why it takes the presentation of our entire body to God. But how could we give less to Him who gave His all for us?

Now we can see why God challenges us to become living sacrifices for Him. It is because of His grace. Our life in God's family should be lived as a response to His grace. Our life should be a big *thank you* to God, not because it is required to earn God's love and acceptance, or because it is required to please others, but to thank God.

So you see, good works are important! Not to earn salvation, but to thank God for salvation. They are not a requirement for eternal life, but should be a result of eternal life.

Out of gratitude for God's grace, we should devote ourselves to doing good in all areas of life. Romans tells us how we can be living sacrifices for Jesus Christ in many other areas.

Your Turn

4. Use a Bible to find and summarize the chief way we can live for Jesus Christ according to each of these passages:

Romans 13:1-7 _____

_____

Romans 13:8-10 _____

_____

Romans 13:11-14 _____

_____

Romans 14:1-23 _____

_____

Romans 15:1-6 _____

_____

When we realize the depth of God's grace to us, we will want to sacrifice our lives in His service. There is no end to the ways we can serve God. We can serve Him anywhere, anytime, and with anybody.

Points to Remember

— God's grace in our salvation should motivate us to respond to Him in gratitude.

— We should present everything to God as a living sacrifice.

— We can then serve Him in many specific ways.

Please Explain...

How should we handle practices over which Christians differ?

Perhaps you noticed that in Romans 14 the writer is discussing how to respond to Christians who differ in certain practices. This is not talking about differences in doctrine, nor is it talking about practices on which the Bible speaks clearly. There are many issues which the Bible does not address clearly or directly, and therefore Christians develop differing opinions. In Romans 14, Christians differed over whether they should eat meat that had been offered to pagan idols, drink wine, and observe certain religious days. Today, good Christians may differ over issues like drinking alcohol, observing Halloween, appropriate movies and music, dancing, and how to dress. These controversial practices are called gray areas or questionable issues because the Bible gives no clear prohibitions or instructions about them. The Bible does, however, give guidelines for how to act towards those who disagree and how to decide if we should participate in a certain activity.

Romans 14 gives some helpful principles in dealing with Christians who differ.

- Accept those who differ without arguing with them (v.1).

- Do not despise or condemn those who differ (v. 3).

- Each person must follow his own convictions (v. 5).

- Whatever you do, do it for the Lord (v. 6).

continued on page 72

How should we handle practices over which Christians differ?

continued from page 71

- Let God judge the other person (v. 10).

- Each person must give an account to God at the Judgment Seat of Christ (v. 12).

- Don't let your activity lead others into sin (v. 13).

- Your choices should always reflect love (v. 15).

- Be a peacemaker (v. 19).

- Do only what builds up others (v. 19).

- Be willing to give up your practice if it hurts another's spiritual life (v. 21).

Another discussion of questionable things appears in 1 Corinthians 8—10. From the summary of that discussion, we distill these questions to use when deciding whether we should participate in an activity.

- Does it edify me or enslave me? (10:23)

- Does it help or hinder other Christians? (10:24)

- Does it glorify God? (10:31)

- Does it weaken my witness to unbelievers? (10:32-33)

Grace frees us, but it frees us to serve God and love others responsibly. We may have the right to do a certain thing, but we also have the freedom to give up that right if it will have a negative impact.

Your Turn

5. When you think of all that God has done for you in salvation, how do you want to thank Him? Write several specific actions you think God may want you to take immediately. You may get some ideas from the verses above, or you may have some specific ideas of your own.

_____

_____

_____

_____

_____

Take It to Heart
Memorize these verses:

Romans 12:1-2 *I beseech you therefore, brethren, by the mercies of God, that you present your bodies a living sacrifice, holy, acceptable to God, which is your reasonable worship. And do not be conformed to this world, but be transformed by the renewing of your mind, that you may prove what is that good and acceptable and perfect will of God.*

There is much more we can say about what it means to serve God as living sacrifices. We will do this in Part III of this study guide. Now that you are a Christian, are sure that you are saved, and want to express your gratitude to God, you will want to continue with Part III to discover how to live the kind of life that pleases God.

Part III: Becoming a Disciple of Jesus Christ

Introduction

When we left our study of Romans, we saw how important it was to respond appropriately to God for all that He has done for us in making us members of His family. There are things we can do with our new life to show our gratitude for all that He has done for us. These things are not to be done to win God's favor—He already has accepted us in Christ. They are done worshipfully as we offer ourselves as "living sacrifices" to God.

When Jesus was on earth, He told those who believed in Him that the ultimate way to serve God was to become a devoted follower of Jesus Christ. This is a way of life open to anyone who will accept the challenge. It is called becoming a disciple. Now we will explore what it means to follow Jesus as a disciple.

First, let's define what a disciple is. The word "disciple" comes from the word "to learn." So a disciple is a learner, or pupil. Sometimes discipleship is referred to as "following" Jesus Christ. That is because a teacher in Jesus' time would gather around himself those who wanted to learn from him and become like him. These pupils would then live with their teacher or master to learn all they could. It was a life devoted to one thing: to become like their master. In the Gospel of Matthew 10:25, Jesus said, *"It is enough for a disciple that he be like his teacher, and a servant like his master."*

Your Turn
In what ways would you like to become like Jesus? List some characteristics of His life you would like to see in yours.

_____

_____

_____

_____

_____

Why should we as Christians want to give our lives to following Christ? Because He gave His life for us. That act of grace deserves our grateful and whole-hearted response. So the first step in becoming a disciple is obviously to become a Christian. Those who accept Christ's invitation to salvation are

---

Please Explain...

What is the difference between salvation and discipleship?

It is important to understand that discipleship is not the same as salvation. Remember that our salvation begins with initial justification, continues in sanctification, and culminates in glorification. Discipleship concerns our sanctification in this life. It is another way of describing committed Christian development and growth into Christlikeness. While there is only one condition for salvation—faith in Christ—there are many conditions for discipleship. This chart will help you see the differences:

Salvation
- Faith in Christ
- Justification
- An instant event
- Free to us
- Works unnecessary
- Christ as Savior
- Coming to Christ

continued on page 74

Discipleship
- Faithfulness to Christ
- Sanctification
- A continual process
- Costly to us
- Works necessary
- Christ as Lord
- Following after Christ

You can see that if we confuse salvation with discipleship, we will make eternal salvation by works instead of faith. Discipleship comes with conditions that are difficult. That is why some Christians do not go on to become true disciples.

One thing is clear, discipleship is God's will for every Christian. Salvation is not the end, but the beginning of a new way of life. The difference between being saved and being a disciple is like the difference between enrolling in a college and showing up for class to barely graduate, and doing all the assignments to get the best education possible and graduate with honors. Once we are saved, God constantly challenges us to new commitments on the road to becoming more of a disciple. We can say that Christians who do not make these commitments are taking a detour from God's will. They have left the path of discipleship. However, they can return to the path by renewing their obedience and commitment.

further invited to follow Him as disciples. We can see Christ giving both invitations in this passage:

"Come to Me, all you who labor and are heavy laden, and I will give you rest. Take My yoke upon you and learn from Me, for I am gentle and lowly in heart, and you will find rest for your souls. For My yoke is easy and My burden is light." (Matthew 11:28-30)

The call to salvation is seen in the invitation to "Come" to Christ. Those who come receive the "rest" of God's righteousness. Jesus' primary audience here is His fellow Jews who were laboring to keep the strenuous man-made demands of their religious leaders, the Scribes and Pharisees, in order to earn eternal life. Of course, this was impossible. Jesus instead offers His righteousness freely, which is a relieving rest from their struggle.

But the call to discipleship is seen in the invitation to "Take My yoke... and learn from Me." To this first century audience, the yoke that bound an ox to a plow was a familiar picture of discipline and obligation. Sometimes a younger animal was trained by yoking it to an older, stronger animal. Jesus invited us to be yoked to Him. He is inviting submission to His teaching and authority as opposed to that of the Scribes and Pharisees. He also promises "rest for your souls." The word "souls" can also be translated "lives." The life of discipleship is a life of peace and rest as we follow God's will instead of our own. It is a delightful way to live because those who commit to following Him find not a heavy burden, but a light and easy load. After all, we are yoked to Jesus and He is the stronger One. Living in partnership with Jesus Christ is always the easiest way to live in the end, because we have the inner delight of serving Him and the resources of the Spirit's power to do His will.

Previously, in Parts I and II, you learned how to relate to Jesus as your Savior and to God as your Father. Now we will learn how to relate to Jesus as your Master and Teacher. But He is not a harsh slave master. As verse 29 above says, Jesus is a Master who is "gentle and lowly in heart." He gives each of His disciples an individually designed load so that they can bear it comfortably and joyfully. Living as Jesus' disciple is the most joyful privilege a child of God has.

Jesus emphasized some essential characteristics of a disciple. These characteristics form the basis for the following lessons. In each lesson you will focus on one characteristic of a disciple that God wants you to develop. Each lesson will discuss what God wants you to know, to do, and to enjoy as a reward for faithfulness in this characteristic.

Lesson 10: Becoming a Devoted Disciple

A Look Back
Explain how what we learned in Romans should motivate us to follow Christ in discipleship and recite the two memory verses from the previous lesson.

_____

_____

_____

A Look Ahead
Disciples commit themselves to the most important relationship in life.

What God Wants You to Know

The first characteristic of a disciple is seen in Jesus' challenge to those who are already believers. He says,

"If anyone comes to Me and does not hate his father and mother, wife and children, brothers and sisters, yes, and even his own life also, he cannot be My disciple." (Luke 14:26)

As we have noticed before, those who "come to" Jesus are those who come to Him to accept His gift of eternal life. They are Christians. But these Christians cannot go on to become true disciples unless they "hate" their family members and even themselves. The word "hate" may seem severe, but it is a figure of speech used in Jesus' day that meant "to love less than." Here Jesus uses it in a positive sense—A disciple must love Him more than his or her own family. Jesus must be the object of one's supreme love and devotion.

This illustration will help you understand how love for one person can look like hate towards others: A man is in a crowded room happily chatting with people who are obviously his friends and family. Suddenly he stands, ignores those still talking to him, turns his back on them and walks quickly toward the door. Does he hate them? No, his fiancée has just entered the room! His full devotion is now trained on her. In comparison to how he loves his fiancée, It looks like he ignores everyone else, even hates them. Of course, he still loves his friends and family, but at that moment it is far less than he loves his wife-to-be.

Your Turn

1. How would you compare the kind of love you have for the Lord with the love you have for your family, spouse, or closest friend?

_____

_____

_____

_____

_____

One very important characteristic of a disciple then is this: A disciple has a supreme and incomparable love for Jesus above and beyond any love towards anyone else. In other words, God wants us to become devoted disciples. Love is more than a feeling. It is a choice and a commitment to devote oneself to another person.

To love God supremely is the first and foremost command for all Christians. Once a Jewish lawyer asked Jesus which was the greatest command (The Old Testament has 613 commands). Jesus answered,
"You shall love the Lord your God with all your heart, with all your soul, and with all your mind. This is the first and great commandment. And the second is like it: 'You shall love your neighbor as yourself.' On these two commandments hang all the law and prophets." (Matthew 22:37-40)

Jesus' answer shows us why loving God above all else is so important for a disciple. First, when we love God supremely, we are engaged in the highest and healthiest activity possible.

Second, we will love others around us. When Jesus says, "the second is like it" He is not referring to a command second in priority, but a second part that cannot be separated from the first. These commands go together like the two halves of a scissors or the two wheels of a bicycle.

Your Turn

2. How are these two commands related and why can't they be separated?

_____

_____

_____

Because of the relationship of these commands, someone has suggested that we only love God as much as we love the person we love the least. In other words, when we love God we love those He loves.

Third, when we love God and others, we keep the commands God has given us through His prophets in the Bible. Obedience, something mandatory for a disciple, is the result of loving God.

One Christian leader put it this way: "Love God and do as you please." He was trying to say that when we love God, we want to please Him, so we will not do anything He does not want us to do.

So when a Christian becomes a disciple exclusively devoted to God, he or she will love others and live a life of obedience. Both these characteristics will be covered in more detail later.

Your Turn
3. What should motivate you to love God supremely?

_____

_____

_____

_____

What God Wants You to Do
The question now is how do we go about loving Jesus? Perhaps that is most easily answered when we look at how we love anyone.

Your Turn
4. How should we think and act toward someone who we really love?

_____

_____

_____

_____

_____

We know that a good marriage is built upon these same things. A man loves a woman and learns to value her, even adore her, which he shows by giving her his attention and gifts. Then he decides to commit himself to her above all other women, so he willingly takes the marriage vows. His greatest desire is to please his lover, so he discovers her desires and tries to fulfill them. His love for her grows as he spends time getting to know her better.

We love Jesus the same way. We will value Him and give to Him our attention and gifts. Let's call this *worship*. We will also commit ourselves to Him above all other commitments or desires. Let's call this *priority*. Then we desire to please Him above all others. Let's call this *obedience*. Finally, we will spend time getting to know Jesus better. Let's call this *communication*. Now we will see what we can do in each of these areas to develop a deeper love.

Your Worship

Worship is what we do to ascribe worth to someone. As a devoted disciple, you will want to let Jesus know what He means to you. An integral part of worship is sacrifice. Under the Old Testament law, the most costly animals were sacrificed by the worshiper to show his devotion. As a living sacrifice, we show how we value God by what we sacrifice to honor Him—our life, time, money, position, etc. We can also worship through prayers, songs sung to God, and praises. An important part of worship is coming together with other people in God's family to pray to God, praise Him, and sing to Him. That is what a church worship service should provide.

Your Turn

5. Think of something that you can give to Jesus that is of great cost to you. What sacrifice can you make to Him?

_____

_____

_____

_____

In what setting will you worship God through prayers, songs, and praises? Are you attending a worship service at a church that encourages this?

_____

_____

_____

Write down two things you can do immediately to enhance your worship of God and His Son.

_____

_____

_____

_____

Your Priority

When we love someone, we put them first. We commit to putting their desires above those of anyone else. Do you have any relationships that require more of your devotion than your relationship to Jesus Christ? For example, do you let a friend talk you into doing something you know would not please God, just so that you remain popular with that friend? Does anyone, anything, or any commitment come before your commitment to doing God's will? How can you make Christ your most important relationship?

Your Turn

6. List the one person, thing, or commitment that threatens to demand more devotion from you than your devotion to the Lord. Now write out how you will keep him, her, or it from getting between you and your relationship with Jesus.

_____

_____

_____

_____

_____

Your Obedience

In a private conversation with His disciples, Jesus told them how to show their love for Him:

"He who has My commandments and keeps them, it is he who loves Me. And he who loves Me will be loved by My Father, and I will love him and manifest Myself to him." (John 14:21)

Are you keeping God's commandments? Do you love Him enough to stop doing things you know He does not want you to do? Do you love Him enough to work on pleasing Him in all areas of your life?

Your Turn

7. List several things you know God wants you to do or stop doing as soon as possible.

_____

_____

_____

_____

_____

Your Communication

It is only natural to want to spend time communicating with those we love. This helps us get to know the person better. Loving Christ means you will spend time communicating with Him. But how? Here are two important ways to get started. First, communicate with God through prayer (Prayer is simply talking to God). Talk to Him honestly about your feelings and needs. Confess your sins to Him. Express your praise and gratitude to Him. Second, read the Bible, since God communicates with us through His Word. Read it daily and frequently to get God's thoughts. (We will say more about reading and studying God's Word in the next lesson.)

Your Turn

8. Explain below what you will do in both of these areas to help your communication with God.

Prayer: _____

_____

_____

Bible Reading: _____

_____

_____

What God Wants You to Enjoy

There are rewards given to disciples who lovingly devote themselves to God.

Note again the promise in the verse we cited earlier:
"He who has My commandments and keeps them, it is he who loves Me. And he who loves Me will be loved by My Father, and I will love him and manifest Myself to him." (John 14:21)

Your Turn

9. What is the promise to those who obey the Lord?

_____

_____

_____

_____

First, when Jesus promises you "will be loved by My Father," He means you will have a greater experience of your Heavenly Father's love. What a wonderful promise this is! The more we obey God, the more we experience His love. To know we are loved and to rest in that love is the greatest experience life has to offer.

Second, when Jesus promises to "manifest" Himself to you, He means that you will have a more intimate fellowship with Him. As in a relationship between two humans, when love grows, so does trust. With trust comes more personal disclosure so that we become a partner to the intimate, sometimes secret, details of a person's life. Jesus is willing to share more of Himself with those who prove through obedience that they are trustworthy.

Friend, do not proceed further in this book without declaring your love for Jesus Christ. Decide now whether you will love Him with all your heart, mind, and soul. Remember, love is not just a feeling; it is more an act of the will expressed in a commitment to serve the desires of someone else. That is why you can _decide_ to love someone. Will you devote yourself to loving God above all other people or things?

Your Turn

10. Take a moment to think about how God loves you and how you should love Him back. Write out your commitment to be devoted to Him in a supreme and loyal love.

_____

_____

_____

_____

_____

_____

_____

Please Explain...

What does the Bible teach about rewards?

Though salvation is a free gift, the Bible teaches that God rewards our worthy works, motives, and sacrifices. Some rewards are enjoyed in this life, and some in eternity (Mark 10:29-30). Jesus said He would reward Christians when He returns (Matthew 16:27).

We may be rewarded with blessings in this life for the things that we do. One reward would be a greater intimacy with Jesus Christ (John 14:21); another is a richer experience of life itself (Matthew 16:25).

Eternal rewards will be bestowed at the Judgment Seat of Christ when we go to be with Christ or when He returns to be with us (2 Corinthians 5:10). This is a judgment of a Christian's works, not a person's salvation. Sometimes the Bible is vague about the nature of eternal rewards. Jesus spoke of "treasures in heaven" without explaining what those treasures were (Matthew 6:20), and New Testament writers spoke of the crown of life (James 1:12), crown of righteousness (2 Timothy 4:8), and crown of glory (1 Peter 5:4) without further explanation. Jesus taught that one clear reward would be participating in the rule of Christ's kingdom as a reward for faithfulness (Luke 19:12-19).

All our deeds, good and bad, will be judged at the Judgment Seat of Christ. Unlike our eternal salvation, potential rewards can be lost by unfaithfulness (Luke 19:2-27), lack of discipline (1 Corinthians 9:24-27), or unworthy motives or deeds (1 Corinthians 3:12-15). It is important for Christians to learn to separate

continued on page 82

Please Explain...

What does the Bible teach about rewards?

continued from page 81

reward passages like these from passages that speak of eternal salvation. If this is not done, eternal salvation becomes conditioned on our faithfulness or good works instead of faith alone.

Sometimes Christians wonder if rewards are a proper motivation for doing good works or serving God. But if God is pleased to bestow them, then they must be good. Besides, rewards can help us glorify God more by allowing us to give more to Him (Revelation 4:10). Rewards are only one motivation for godliness, but they show us that as Christians we will be held accountable for how we use our lives.

Points to Remember

— God wants you to become a devoted disciple.

— Devotion means you have a supreme and incomparable love for Jesus Christ.

— We can love Him by worshiping Him, making Him our priority, obeying Him, and spending time communicating with Him.

— Jesus gives those who love and obey Him a deeper experience of God's love and His own life.

Take It to Heart
Memorize these verses:

Matthew 22:37-40 *Jesus said to him, "You shall love the Lord your God with all your heart, with all your soul, and with all your mind. This is the first and great commandment. And the second is like it: 'You shall love your neighbor as yourself.' On these two commandments hang all the law and prophets."*

John 14:21 *He who has My commandments and keeps them, it is he who loves Me. And he who loves Me will be loved by My Father, and I will love him and manifest Myself to him.*

This first lesson of Part III taught you that God wants you to become a devoted disciple. As we have seen, this involves a supreme loyal love for Jesus. In the next lesson, you will discover more about how that love is expressed in obedience to Him.

Lesson 11: Becoming an Obedient Disciple

A Look Back
Explain what it means to have a supreme and incomparable love for Jesus Christ and how you practiced that this past week. Recite the two memory verses from the previous lesson.

_____

_____

_____

A Look Ahead
Disciples learn to obey what God says.

What God Wants You to Know

Another characteristic of discipleship is found in John 8:

Then Jesus said to those Jews who believed Him, "If you abide in My word, you are My disciples indeed. And you shall know the truth, and the truth will make you free." (John 8:31-32)

Your Turn
1. How is the condition for being a disciple stated here?

_____

_____

_____

What does the "If" imply?

_____

_____

_____

Again, we notice that this is a challenge to those "who believed Him," therefore, they are Christians. The word "abide" means to "remain in" or "continue in." It denotes the closest relationship to something. For example, a dead wooden stake can be driven into the earth and no growth will take place, but a tomato seedling planted in the earth will grow and bear fruit. The plant is not just *in* the earth, but has a relationship that is so close and dependent on the earth, that it draws sustenance and strength from the earth. So *abide* implies a close relationship to, adherence to, or obedience to the Word of God. God wants us to be obedient disciples as we make ourselves living sacrifices to Him.

Now we see how the Bible is crucial to a life of discipleship. It is in the Bible that God reveals His will for us. We can trust the Bible as God's Word to us. A key passage makes several claims about God's Word:
All Scripture is given by inspiration of God, and is profitable for doctrine, for reproof, for correction, for instruction in righteousness, that the man of God may be complete, thoroughly equipped for every good work.
(2 Timothy 3:16-17)

Please Explain...

How do we know the Bible is without error?

The idea of inspiration guarantees that there are no errors in the Bible. The easiest way to show this is to ask someone to find one. No one can. Most things that may appear contradictory will be resolved with further study. There are many books devoted to explaining these difficult Bible verses. There is other evidence that the Bible is without error:

- Portions are quoted authoritatively by Jesus, Paul, and other writers of Scripture.

- Hundreds of prophecies have been fulfilled already.

- Bible has outlasted all its critics to remain the most popular book in the world.

Technically, the inspiration and the inerrancy (i.e., having no errors) of the Bible apply only to the original documents. Since we no longer have them, but only copies, you may wonder how we know they are accurate copies. This is easy to

continued on page 85

Your Turn
2. What are the claims made about God's Word in this passage?

_____

_____

_____

_____

_____

The first claim uses the word "inspiration," which literally means "God-breathed." It refers to the process by which God delivered His Word through the original writers. Though every Bible author reflects his personal characteristics in His writing, inspiration means that the end result is exactly what God wants to say. This means that the Bible is without error as it was originally written.

The second claim of 2 Timothy 3:16-17 is that the Bible is "profitable." For what is it profitable? Put a number by each of the following four things in the verse:
1) For *doctrine*. That is another word for teaching. God teaches us His truth in the Bible. For example, it tells us about His will, His character, His saving work, and His plans for the future. Its teaching is the final authority in determining truth.
2) For *reproof*. The Bible not only tells us what is right, but what is wrong. When we do wrong, the Bible confronts us with the truth about our behavior.
3) For *correction*. The Bible not only tells us when we are doing wrong, it helps us get back on the right course. It corrects our behavior.

4) For *instruction in righteousness*. The Bible shows us how to live an upright life.

The third claim of this passage is the result of taking the Bible seriously: We will be "complete" and "equipped for every good work." The Bible prepares us in knowledge, character, and conduct. The more we know the Bible, the more completely equipped we are to serve God and others by our good works.

Your Turn

3. In which area do you feel the greatest need to be equipped: knowledge, character, or conduct? Why?

_____

_____

_____

_____

Now you see why Jesus said that a disciple must continue in His Word. That is where our Master Jesus communicates His will for us and equips us for life. But there is a crucial aspect to continuing in God's Word. When we discover His will in His Word, we must obey it. If we do not, our study of the Bible is only an academic exercise.

What God Wants You to Do

God did not give us the Bible to make us smart, but to change our lives. We change as we obey and apply its truths. To be an obedient disciple, we must do three things with God's Word:

First, we must *spend time in it*. Christians who are growing to be like Christ have a regular habit of reading and studying God's Word. It is through the Word that we come to know Christ better. You can read a few verses a day, or much more. What is important is the regular "feeding" on the Word. It is easiest for newer Christians to begin reading the New Testament, preferably in one of the Gospels like Mark or John. From there, one might want to read the New Testament epistles (letters), or the foundational Old Testament book of Genesis. Psalms and Proverbs offer a lot of encouragement and wisdom for life.

Please Explain...

How do we know the Bible is without error?

continued from page 84

answer. We have copies of much of the Old Testament that are 2000 years old. When we compare them to today's versions, we see that accuracy has been preserved through the centuries. Though some of the Old Testament was written 1500 years before these oldest copies, we can assume they were copied just as carefully then also. We have even more copies of the New Testament (over 5000). Some copies are portions of the New Testament which date back to the 2nd century A.D. The New Testament was completed near the end of the 1st century A.D., so there is not much of a gap. These portions, as well as later complete manuscripts, show us that the Bible has been copied faithfully with extreme accuracy. Even though it has been translated many times into many different languages, we can trust the accuracy of the Bible as if it were God's original Word to us. God has seen to it that we have His true words.

Your Turn

4. As a disciple, you need a regular time set aside to be in the Bible. This is not just a ritual, but a way of deepening your fellowship with God as you meet Him in His Word. It may not be very long at first, but try to spend as much time as possible. Write out a plan that will help you get started spending time with God in the Bible:

When will I read it during the day?: _____

_____

Where will I do my reading?: _____

_____

What book will I read first?: _____

_____

When will I begin?: _____

_____

Second, we must *learn to understand it*. We should approach the Bible with a desire to understand what it means. It is helpful to use a pen, colored pencils, or other markers to underline or circle things that are significant to you. You should learn to ask key questions about a passage such as: To whom was it written? Why was it written? What does it say?, and What does it mean? Here are some more suggestions for understanding the Bible:

— *Pray.* Since the truth of the Bible is taught and applied by the Holy Spirit, why not get in the habit of asking Him for help?

— *Seek the ordinary meaning.* When you read, use your common sense like you would with any other book. Recognize figures of speech when they occur and take things literally when they are obviously meant to be so.

— *Be aware of the context.* Nothing is written in a vacuum, but every verse comes in a context. Usually things said before and after a verse will help you understand the meaning of a difficult verse. Out of context, verses can be twisted or used to say anything.

— *Learn backgrounds.* The more you can learn about ancient history, language, culture, religion, etc., the richer your Bible study will be.

— *Interpret difficult passages in light of the easier ones.* If a verse is hard to understand, other easier ones may cast light on it for you.

— *Consult books about the Bible.* There are many books (called commentaries) available that explain Bible passages. Caution: Some are better than others, and none is perfect. Bible dictionaries and lexicons can help you understand individual words.

— *Recognize important differences in the Bible.* There are different authors, types of literature, purposes for various Bible books, time periods, and ways in which God worked through the various time periods.

You can see why Bible study can become a life-long activity! So don't let your lack of knowledge or experience discourage you. You will usually find something you can understand and apply no matter where you are studying. Use what you can understand and be patient with the rest.

Your Turn

5. An important part of Bible study is learning to ask good questions about the verse being studied. Read and think about the verse below. What questions would you ask in order to understand what this verse means? Write your questions below the verse.

"But you shall receive power when the Holy Spirit has come upon you; and you shall be witnesses to Me in Jerusalem, and in all Judea and Samaria, and to the end of the earth." (Acts 1:8)

_____

_____

_____

_____

_____

_____

Third, we must *apply it*. This should be the result of all Bible study. Though there is only one interpretation of a passage, there can be many applications. We must do whatever we discover God wants us to do. A good way to come up with applications is to ask yourself the following questions about what the passage says:

—*Do I need to change an attitude?*

—*Do I need to stop doing something?*

—*Do I need to start doing something?*

Your Turn

6. Those who seriously apply the Bible's truths come up with a plan they can follow. Read the verse below and write out a plan explaining how you can turn these truths into actions. Include how you will do it, with whom, when you will do it, and other specific details.

And be kind to one another, tender-hearted, forgiving one another, even as God in Christ forgave you. (Ephesians 4:32)

_____

_____

_____

_____

_____

_____

_____

_____

What God Wants You to Enjoy

The condition for becoming a disciple cited at the beginning of this lesson comes with a promise. Look at the verses again:

Then Jesus said to those Jews who believed Him, "If you abide in My word, you are My disciples indeed. And you shall know the truth, and the truth will make you free." (John 8:31-32)

Your Turn

7. What is the promise?

_____

_____

_____

Jesus then explains the promise in more detail:

Jesus answered them, "Most assuredly, I say to you, whoever commits sin is a slave of sin. And a slave does not abide in the house forever, but a son abides forever. Therefore if the Son makes you free, you shall be free indeed. (John 8:34-36)

Your Turn

8. What are we freed from?

_____

_____

_____

What are some sins that easily enslave people?

_____

_____

_____

_____

_____

_____

The truth of God's Word frees us from the deception of error that will lead to incorrect beliefs or behavior. It frees us from sin that comes from ignorance of His will. It also teaches us to walk in His will so that we can avoid further sin. Slaves are restricted in privilege, but children of God have freedom to enjoy their relationship to God as Father and Jesus as Master.

Freedom is not a life without boundaries. True freedom is knowing and appreciating our boundaries. For example, a train is free to run when it is on railroad tracks. If it frees itself from the tracks, it becomes bogged down in mud. Likewise, a fish is free in its intended environment, the water. But if it asserts its freedom to come up on land, it will die. Imagine a country without rules. There would not be freedom, but anarchy that leads to the slavery of fear. The Bible tells us that the boundaries for enjoying life in the fullest is God's will revealed in the Bible.

The more you learn to read, study, and obey the Bible, the more you will enjoy a life of freedom from the slavery to sin and its companion guilt. You will be free to relate to God as your Father and enjoy an intimate walk with Jesus as your Master.

Obedience to God's Word is not an option for the growing disciple. You must decide now whether you will obey what you read in the Bible. Can you sincerely say, "Whatever He says, I will do"? Can you say that to God now?

Your Turn

9. Name one area of your life where you can easily be deceived or enslaved by sin, then explain how you can obey God and find freedom in this area.

_____

_____

_____

_____

_____

_____

Sometimes it's not easy to obey. But just remember that there is always a blessing from obedience. God rewards His obedient children with a glorious freedom; a freedom from slavery to sin and the negative effects of its consequences!

Points to Remember

— God wants you to become an obedient disciple who continues in His Word.

—This means you will spend time in it, learn to understand it, and apply it.

— Jesus promises a life of true freedom for those who obey His Word.

Take It to Heart
Memorize these verses:

John 8:31-32 _Then Jesus said to those Jews who believed Him, "If you abide in My word, you are My disciples indeed. And you shall know the truth, and the truth will make you free."_

2 Timothy 3:16-17 _All Scripture is given by inspiration of God, and is profitable for doctrine, for reproof, for correction, for instruction in righteousness, that the man of God may be complete, thoroughly equipped for every good work._

You have now studied two very important characteristics of a disciple: an exclusive love for Jesus, and obedience to His Word. Continue with the next lesson to discover a third characteristic of a disciple.

Lesson 12: Becoming a Selfless Disciple

A Look Back
Explain the relationship a disciple should have to God's Word and how you practiced that this past week. Recite the two memory verses from the previous lesson.

_____

_____

_____

A Look Ahead
Disciples learn to deny their own desires in order to do God's will.

What God Wants You to Know

We now turn to a passage that mentions three more characteristics for discipleship stated as conditions. Jesus is speaking to his disciples:
Then He said to them all, "If anyone desires to come after Me, let him deny himself, and take up his cross daily, and follow Me." (Luke 9:23)

Your Turn
1. What are the three conditions in this verse for following Christ as a disciple?

1. _____

2. _____

3. _____

Here Jesus is inviting His disciples (the nearest identity of "them all" in this verse is the twelve disciples mentioned in verse 18) to follow Him in a greater commitment of discipleship. These men were already following Jesus, but Jesus gives them a greater challenge. This is not unusual. Jesus always challenges a disciple to become more of a disciple. There is always a greater commitment that challenges us to grow. Discipleship is a journey, not a destination.

Jesus uses the phrase "come after me." This refers to following Him in a life of discipleship. This is different from the phrase we encountered earlier, "Come to me," which refers to approaching Jesus for eternal life through faith.

In this section of our study, we will focus only on the first of the three conditions mentioned in this one verse: "let him deny himself." Jesus is saying that a disciple is characterized by a selfless attitude. It is an attitude that denies one's own desires to fulfill God's desires. In other words, a disciple says "no" to self and "yes" to God. God's will takes precedence over our own, because as a living sacrifice, we have given up our own will for His.

Your Turn

2. What things do you think Jesus' original twelve disciples had to deny themselves in order to follow Him as pupils? (Maybe you can relate this to the sacrifices made today by someone who goes back to college after starting a career and family; similar circumstances to what these twelve disciples faced.) Write down some things you think of.

_____

_____

_____

_____

_____

_____

Giving preference to God's desires over our own is a constant struggle for the disciple. Our sinful self does not naturally want what God wants. There is a constant war going on between our selfish desires and what God wants. Another passage that shows this is in the New Testament book of Galatians: _I say then: Walk in the Spirit, and you shall not fulfill the lust of the flesh. For the flesh lusts against the Spirit, and the Spirit against the flesh; and these are contrary to one another, so that you do not do the things that you wish._ (Galatians 5:16-17)

Your Turn

3. According to these verses, how can we prevent giving in to our lusts and desires?

_____

_____

_____

"Walking in the Spirit" comes by focusing on the things of the Spirit instead of our selfish desires. Just as Romans 8:1-11 told us, the only way to get the victory over our sinful desires is to allow the Holy Spirit within us to over-power our desires in favor of God's desires. Similarly, Galatians 5:16-17 is saying that if we focus on the Spirit, we will do what He desires. We will not fulfill our selfish desires, some of which are listed in the verses that follow: *Now the works of the flesh are evident, which are: adultery, fornication, un-cleanness, licentiousness, idolatry, sorcery, hatred, contentions, jealousies, outbursts of wrath, selfish ambitions, dissensions, heresies, envy, murder, drunkenness, revelries, and the like...* (Galatians 5:19-21a)

(Some definitions might be helpful: *Uncleanness* can be any kind of immorality, but is usually used in reference to sexual sins. *Licentiousness* refers to unashamed sensual or sexual excesses. *Revelries* is rowdy carousing and partying.)

Your Turn

4. Which of these sins do you need to be rid of most?

_____

_____

_____

When we live to please the Holy Spirit, we will not only deny ourselves these sinful things, but we will experience what the Spirit produces in us: *But the fruit of the Spirit is love, joy, peace, longsuffering, kindness, good-ness, faithfulness, gentleness, self-control...* (Galatians 5:22-23a)

Your Turn

5. Which of the fruit of the Spirit do you most need to see more of in your life?

_____

_____

_____

To see how the Spirit helps us deny ourselves, let's use a couple of examples. First, suppose you are offered a new prestigious position with a company that also gives you an opportunity to make a lot of money selling a product, but you would have to lie about the capabilities of that product. However, you know that lying would not be pleasing to God. To please the Holy Spirit, you decline the job, denying yourself more money and prestige. In this case, you have avoided one of the sins listed earlier, "selfish ambition." Instead you find that God has given you a new experience of His love, joy, and peace—the fruit of walking in the Spirit.

Another example might be when someone criticizes you unfairly. You really want to tell him what you think of him, but you know that is not what God wants you to do. So with the Spirit's help you stay quiet. You have avoided being "contentious" and having "outbursts of wrath." Instead, God's Spirit is producing His fruit of longsuffering, kindness, and self-control in you.

God wants us to become selfless disciples who are given to do His will at the expense of our own.

What God Wants You to Do

You can evaluate your selflessness by going through the list of sinful behaviors and attitudes listed in Galatians 5:19-21a above. In each of these, ask yourself whether you are giving in to your own desires, or denying yourself selfish pleasure in order to do God's will. For example, the first sins mentioned are adultery (sexual immorality that violates the sanctity of marriage vows) and fornication (more general sexual immorality). If married, have you been tempted to be unfaithful to your spouse physically and sexually? If not married, have you kept yourself sexually pure? Or since you know that adultery and fornication are wrong, have you submitted to God's Spirit and denied yourself the temporary pleasure of such a sin? Furthermore, are you tempted to even imagine or fantasize an adulterous or immoral relationship? Or do you deny yourself these unclean thoughts so that your mind might be pleasing to God?

Your Turn

6. Look at the other sinful behaviors in the list from Galatians 5:19-21a above. Find one that is a present source of temptation for you and write out what it means to say no to yourself and yes to God in this area.

How I say "No" to my own desire   How I say "Yes" to God's desire

_____   _____

_____   _____

_____   _____

_____   _____

What God Wants You to Enjoy

There is a promise tucked into these verses from Galatians 5 that we should not miss. It is stated at the end of the list of sinful behaviors:

...of which I told you beforehand, just as I also told you in time past, that those who practice such things will not inherit the kingdom of God. (Galatians 5:21b)

Your Turn

7. Though stated negatively, what is the implied positive promise?

_____

_____

_____

Though this verse may simply be a warning not to behave like unbelievers who are not entering God's kingdom, some think it says that those who deny themselves selfish desires will not only *enter* the kingdom of God (a free gift given to all who believe in Christ for eternal salvation), but they will also *inherit* the kingdom of God (a reward earned by subsequent faithfulness). You may recall that in Romans 8:17 we saw that those who suffered with Christ in overcoming sin through the Spirit are called "joint heirs with Christ" because they will inherit the glory of Christ's future kingdom. This is the same idea. If we deny ourselves, we will be rewarded with a greater experience in Christ's coming kingdom. We may lose a temporary pleasure in this life, but we will gain eternal privileges in the future life.

Jesus made the same promise to His disciples who had left all to follow Him. They had denied themselves the pleasure of their homes and families, their occupations and security—everything! A conversation between Peter and Jesus helps us understand the promise of a future inheritance implied in Galatians:

Then Peter answered and said to Him, "See, we have left all and followed You. Therefore what shall we have?" (Matthew 19:27)

Peter knew what he had denied himself in order to follow Jesus and is evidently wondering whether it is really worth it. Jesus consoles Peter and all the disciples with this answer:

So Jesus said to them, "Assuredly I say to you, that in the regeneration, when the Son of Man sits on the throne of His glory, you who have followed Me will also sit on the twelve thrones, judging the twelve tribes of Israel. And everyone who has left houses or brothers or sisters or father or mother or wife or children or lands, for My name's sake, shall receive a hundredfold, and inherit everlasting life." (Matthew 19:28-29)

8. List the various aspects of Jesus' promised rewards.

_____

_____

_____

_____

_____

_____

_____

_____

Jesus uses the word "regeneration" to refer to the future time of God's kingdom on earth when the earth will be renovated. Those who deny themselves even good things like a home, or family, or wealth to do God's will, will be repaid "a hundredfold." This is probably a figure of speech that means "many times over" and refers to a multiplied sense of God's provision. The Gospel of Mark and the Gospel of Luke make it clear in their accounts of this same conversation that this reward begins in this "present time" (Mark 10:30; Luke 18:30). This is part of the abundant life we discussed in Part I of this study guide. But those who deny themselves will also be allowed to participate in Jesus' glorious rule in His future kingdom. For the twelve apostles, that meant ruling over the twelve tribes of Israel. Jesus describes our participation with the phrase "inherit everlasting life." To be an _heir_ is to have legal ownership, but to _inherit_ is to have actual possession. Jesus is not talking about how to obtain eternal life initially (salvation, justification), but how to enjoy that life eternally. To inherit eternal life means that we are given the privilege of enjoying to the fullest that which is legally ours.

Your Turn

9. How would you compare the significance of a reward in this life with a reward in eternity?

_____

_____

_____

_____

So you see, there is reward for those who deny themselves. We don't end up with less, but more. When we deny ourselves, our pleasure may be diminished for a moment, but it is enhanced both in this life and for eternity. Whatever you deny yourself in this life will be repaid in a multiplied abundance of God's blessings both now and forever. It pays to serve God! It pays to sacrifice for Him! It pays to deny ourselves for His sake!

Your Turn

10. How does this promise motivate you to follow through on your commitment to say *no* to yourself and *yes* to God in the temptation you named from the list in Galatians 5:19-21a?

_____

_____

_____

_____

It is so easy to hold tightly to the pleasures of this life. But we must believe Christ's promise that whenever we say *no* to self and *yes* to God, we will increase the real pleasures of this life as well as those in the future life in the kingdom.

Jesus Christ denied Himself His glory in heaven and His own life for you. In responding to Him as a living sacrifice, have you sacrificed your own desires for His? What is He asking you to deny yourself for His sake right now? Will you say *no* to yourself? Never hesitate to say *yes* to Jesus!

Points to Remember

— God wants you to become a selfless disciple.

— You become a selfless disciple by denying yourself—renouncing your own selfish desires to do God's will instead.

— If you do this, God will give you a rich experience in this life and the future kingdom.

Take It to Heart

Memorize these verses:

Luke 9:23 *Then He said to them all, "If anyone desires to come after Me, let him deny himself, and take up his cross daily, and follow Me."*

Galatians 5:22-23 *But the fruit of the Spirit is love, joy, peace, longsuffering, kindness, goodness, faithfulness, gentleness, self-control. Against such there is no law.*

You are doing well to make it through this important lesson! Our next lesson will explain another one of Jesus' characteristics for discipleship.

Lesson 13: Becoming a Suffering Disciple

 A Look Back
Explain what it means to be a selfless disciple and give an example of how you denied yourself this past week. Recite the two memory verses from the previous lesson.

_____

_____

_____

A Look Ahead
Disciples must be willing to suffer for their identification with Jesus Christ.

What God Wants You to Know

No one likes to suffer, but this too is a part of being a disciple. Suffering is implied in our role as living sacrifices. It is the second of the three conditions mentioned in Luke 9:23.

Then He said to them all, "If anyone desires to come after Me, let him deny himself, and take up his cross daily, and follow Me."

It is mentioned again in Luke 14:27:

"And whoever does not bear his cross and come after Me cannot be My disciple."

Your Turn
1. Does mention of the "cross" stir any negative thoughts or feelings in you? Explain.

_____

_____

_____

_____

To be a disciple, one must "take up his cross daily." But what does this mean? You know that Jesus died on the cross and that for Him it meant great suffering. The disciples had not yet seen Jesus die on the cross, but they were familiar with the practice of Roman crucifixion. It was the cruelest and most inhumane method of execution. A condemned person was required to publicly carry his own cross beam to the place of crucifixion. After this humiliation, he was tied and nailed to the cross beam which was then tied and nailed to the upright beam. Dying on the cross was slow and painful. Eventually, the convict usually suffocated from the sagging weight of his body, which prevented him from breathing.

Your Turn

2. What feelings do you think the disciples might have had when Jesus mentioned the cross?

_____

_____

_____

_____

Surely when Jesus said a disciple must take up his cross, the disciples felt a shudder of horror. Jesus was asking them to bear humiliation and even physical suffering for His sake. Would they be willing?

There are different kinds of suffering. We may suffer the consequences of our or another's sin. Or we may suffer physically from poor health or finances. But this fourth characteristic of discipleship addresses suffering that comes from our identity as disciples of Jesus Christ.

In another passage of the Bible, Jesus warned His followers that they would suffer persecution:
"If the world hates you, you know that it hated Me before it hated you. If you were of the world, the world would love its own. Yet because you are not of the world, but I chose you out of the world, therefore the world hates you. Remember the word that I said to you, 'A servant is not greater than his master.' If they persecuted Me, they will also persecute you. If they kept My word, they will keep yours also. But all these things they will do to you for My name's sake, because they do not know Him who sent Me."
(John 15:18-21)

Your Turn

3. Who or what do you think "the world" refers to?

_____

_____

_____

Living in the Family of Grace

Why do you think the world hates Christ and His followers?

_____

_____

_____

_____

To be identified with Jesus Christ will certainly cause suffering for the Christian in this world, because the world of humanity in its natural unsaved condition is opposed to Christ. Its values and ideas are contrary to His. To some degree or other we will suffer to follow Christ.

For almost 2000 years people have had to suffer for following Christ. Many were put to death just because they were Christians. Even today in some countries Christians are ostracized, harassed, beaten, abused, and even killed. Living sacrifices sometimes die from their devotion to Jesus Christ.

We may not only suffer persecution from others, but we may suffer from the consequences of denying ourselves in order to do God's will. If we turn down a prestigious well-paying job because it would cause us to compromise God's will, then we may suffer financial hardship, ridicule from friends, or the scorn of a spouse. If an employee refuses to cheat on a progress report, he may be passed up for a promotion. If a woman chooses to wait until marriage to lose her virginity, she may lose friends and social opportunities.

So the fourth characteristic of a disciple is the willingness to suffer in our identity as a Christian and follower of Christ. God wants us to be willing to suffer for Him as His disciples.

Notice something else Jesus said in Luke 9:23: He said that a disciple must take up his cross "daily." This refers to a continual conscious willingness to identify with Christ regardless of consequences. We may endure suffering and persecution one day, only to find that the next day has its own challenges.

What God Wants You to Do

Maybe you have already had occasions when you were tempted to hide your Christian identity. Perhaps you were reluctant to tell a family member or friend that you had become a Christian. Maybe you compromised your behavior so you wouldn't stand out too much from everyone else.

Your Turn

4. Have you ever had a negative reaction when you told someone you were a Christian or that you believed the Bible, or when you chose not to participate in something sinful others wanted you to do? Explain.

_____

_____

_____

_____

God wants you to unashamedly identify with Him. Do your family, friends, employer, co-workers, teacher, students, or neighbors know that you are a Christian? Sometimes it is wise to wait for the right time, the right place, and the right way to tell them, but eventually you should let them know.

Or perhaps you fear reprisal from choosing a Christian course of conduct. When we follow Christ in our home, community, or work place, we will eventually clash with the popular but non-Christian morality. Are you willing to do what is right despite the cost and suffering it may cause you?

Your Turn

5. Name a present situation where it will cause you some suffering or ridicule to be identified as a Christian. Have you taken up your cross in this situation? Explain, then pause to pray for God's strength and wisdom in dealing with it.

_____

_____

_____

What God Wants You to Enjoy

While Jesus told His followers to expect suffering, He also assured them of certain blessings in their suffering. In what is called The Sermon on the Mount, Jesus preached these words of consolation:

"Blessed are those who are persecuted for righteousness' sake, for theirs is the kingdom of heaven. Blessed are you when they revile and persecute you, and say all kinds of evil against you falsely for My sake. Rejoice and be exceedingly glad, for great is your reward in heaven, for so they persecuted the prophets who were before you." (Matthew 5:10-12)

Your Turn

6. What is the consolation Jesus mentions?

_____

_____

_____

_____

What attitude does Jesus expect when we are persecuted?

_____

_____

_____

_____

Later, as Jesus' twelve disciples were preparing to go out and preach to people about Him, He encouraged them with these words:

"And do not fear those who kill the body but cannot kill the soul. But rather fear Him who is able to destroy both body and soul in hell. Are not two sparrows sold for a copper coin? And not one of them falls to the ground apart from your Father's will. But the very hairs of your head are all numbered. Do not fear, therefore; you are of more value than the sparrows." (Matthew 10:28-31)

Your Turn

7. How does Jesus minimize the fear of physical harm?

_____

_____

_____

_____

Though physical harm may kill the body, we should never worry about our soul (a word the Bible often uses to refer to our essential life). Our real life is in safe keeping with Christ Himself. Our fear of God should exceed our fear of anyone else. His power is unlimited while other people are limited in what they can do to us. Besides, when we suffer, God knows about it and cares for us. He will not let anything happen to us that is not part of His purpose. If God cares about sparrows, He certainly cares more about us!

But Jesus continues His encouragement of the twelve disciples with both a word about a reward and a warning:

"Therefore whoever confesses Me before men, him I will also confess before My Father who is in heaven. But whoever denies Me before men, him I will also deny before My Father who is in heaven." (Matthew 10:32-33)

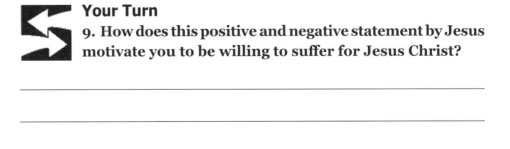

Your Turn

8. What is the positive reward and what do you think it means?

_____

_____

_____

What is the negative consequence and what do you think it means?

_____

_____

_____

The disciples would soon be out preaching. When threatened with persecution for their message they might be tempted to deny their relationship to Jesus. But Jesus promises them a reward when they admit their relationship to Him. Jesus will "confess" them before God the Father. While the significance of the confession is not fully explained, it is spoken of positively and suggests both Christ's approval and the Father's approval. It even hints of a reward based on that approval.

Similarly, He warns the disciples that whoever denies Him before others, He will deny before the Father. This is not talking about eternal salvation being denied. We do not earn salvation by confessing Christ, nor lose it by denying Him to others. Again, the warning is not specific in its details, but certainly God's disapproval is expressed. Also, those who deny Christ may be denied rewards such as a greater role in the kingdom.

Your Turn

9. How does this positive and negative statement by Jesus motivate you to be willing to suffer for Jesus Christ?

_____

_____

_____

Isn't it a comfort to know that when we are called to suffer, we are promised rewards that out-weigh what others may do to us? Yes, suffering because of our relationship with Christ may not be pleasant to think about or experience. But when we take up this cross each day, it should remind us of Jesus who faced the most horrible form of suffering for us. With His example and love to motivate us, and His promised rewards to console us, should we hesitate to accept suffering for Him? If we are truly living sacrifices, we will feel privileged to suffer for the One who suffered so much for us.

Points to Remember

— God wants you to become a suffering disciple.

— We must constantly commit ourselves to following Jesus despite the consequences.

— Jesus consoles us in suffering with promises of God's approval and rewards.

Take It to Heart
Memorize these verses:

Matthew 5:10-12 *"Blessed are those who are persecuted for righteousness' sake, for theirs is the kingdom of heaven. Blessed are you when they revile and persecute you, and say all kinds of evil against you falsely for My sake. Rejoice and be exceedingly glad, for great is your reward in heaven, for so they persecuted the prophets who were before you."*

You are now ready to see another characteristic of a disciple. It is the third part of this same verse, Luke 9:23. Please continue with the next lesson.

Lesson 14: Becoming a Submissive Disciple

 A Look Back
Explain how disciples may suffer for Jesus Christ and how you may have experienced this characteristic of a disciple this past week. Recite the two memory verses from the previous lesson.

_____

_____

_____

A Look Ahead
Disciples submit to God's purpose for their lives.

What God Wants You to Know

As you read Luke 9:23 again, underline the third condition of discipleship in this verse.

Then He said to them all, "If anyone desires to come after Me, let him deny himself, and take up his cross daily, and follow Me."

Jesus' words are simply "follow Me." On the surface, this looks like a simple invitation to tag along with Jesus. But the way a person of Jesus' time would have understood it was more involved. It was understood as an invitation to become one of His pupils or disciples. As mentioned in the introduction to Part III, ancient teachers would gather around themselves those who wanted to learn what they taught and become what they were. So if someone enlisted as a disciple, he was agreeing to something like an apprenticeship. It was a relationship of submission to a master who would teach him.

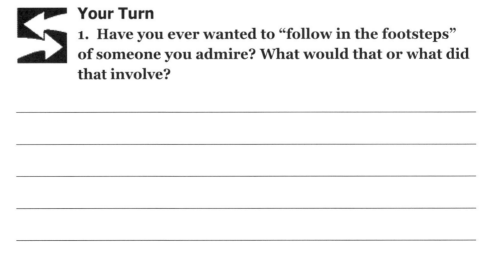 **Your Turn**
1. Have you ever wanted to "follow in the footsteps" of someone you admire? What would that or what did that involve?

_____

_____

_____

_____

God wants you to become a submissive disciple. As such, you will be characterized by a willingness to go where Jesus leads and learn what Jesus teaches. This is really the essence of discipleship. Remember Jesus' words in Matthew 11:29: *"Take my yoke upon you and learn from me."*

It should go without saying that a disciple is one who has a teachable attitude. This is an attitude that submits to a teacher of higher authority. If we are not submissive, we are not teachable.

Though Jesus was with His first disciples only three years, discipleship is really a life-long process of learning. We never stop learning, so we never should stop being a submissive disciple.

What Jesus taught His disciples was not merely doctrinal truth. He also taught them things like how to minister to others, how to trust God for their needs, and their purpose in life. Sometimes He taught by words, sometimes by example. Probably more was *caught* from His example than was *taught* by His words.

What God Wants You to Do

There are many things to learn as a follower of Jesus Christ. One of the first things Jesus taught His disciples was their purpose in life. Every Christian ought to know his or her purpose in life.

Your Turn
2. Have you ever thought about your purpose in life? How would you explain to someone what that purpose is?

_____

_____

_____

_____

In general, we could say that our purpose in life is to glorify God. But specifically how do we do that? Did Jesus tell us a more specific purpose we were to have as His submissive disciples? He certainly did!

See if you catch Christ's purpose for the disciples in this invitation to His first disciples to follow Him:

And Jesus, walking by the Sea of Galilee, saw two brothers, Simon called Peter, and Andrew his brother, casting a net into the sea; for they were fishermen. And He said to them, "Follow Me, and I will make you fishers of men." Then they immediately left their nets and followed Him.
(Matthew 4:18-20)

 Your Turn
3. How would you state Christ's purpose for these disciples?

_____

_____

_____

When Jesus promised to make these disciples fishers of men, He was talking about using them to spread the good news of His salvation so that people would believe and be gathered into the family of God. There's quite a difference between catching fish for food and catching people for God's family. Only the latter has eternal significance.

Spreading the gospel to others so that they might be saved is called *evangelism.* Sometimes it is called *witnessing,* because we tell others what we know about Jesus Christ or what we have experienced as a Christian. Winning people to Himself was always Jesus' priority when He was on earth. We see in other places in the Bible that it also became the priority for His disciples. Jesus did indeed make them fishers of men. They later brought thousands into the family of God!

Why is bringing people to Christ for salvation such a priority? Well, think about all the Christian activities a person can engage in: worship, prayer, Bible study, helping others, etc. All of these things can be done when we are in heaven! Only one thing will be impossible—evangelism! God wants us to win people to Christ in this life because it is the only opportunity to do so.

 Your Turn
4. Of all the Christian activities you engage in, how much of a priority has it been in your life to try to bring people to Christ?

_____

_____

This is so important to Jesus that His last words to His disciples before He ascended into heaven charged them with this responsibility:

"All authority has been given to Me in heaven and on earth. Go therefore and make disciples of all the nations, baptizing them in the name of the Father and of the Son and of the Holy Spirit, teaching them to observe all things that I have commanded you; and lo, I am with you always, even to the end of the age." (Matthew 28:18-20)

In the passage above, underline the commands.

This command is sometimes called "The Great Commission" because it so forcefully and clearly states what Jesus wants us as disciples to do. The original wording shows that the main command in this commission is "make disciples." We do that by *going, baptizing, and teaching.* Let's consider each of these three things separately.

Go
The way this word is used in this verse, it means "as you are going." People cannot become disciples unless someone goes to them and tells them about the saving work of Jesus Christ. The first step in becoming a disciple is obviously to become a Christian. Non-Christians cannot possibly be true disciples.

Your Turn
5. **What are some obstacles that keep Christians from going to others to share the gospel message?**

_____

_____

_____

_____

Baptize
After becoming a Christian, a person should get baptized as soon as possible. When a person is baptized they are immersed in water as a way of identifying with Jesus Christ. Baptism shows others what has already happened invisibly: God's Holy Spirit has given new birth and has placed us into the invisible body of Christ forever. So it is an outward symbol of an inner reality. Baptism is usually done by a church or in a church to show that the person is also identifying with God's people.

Please Explain...

What does the Bible teach about how a person should be baptized?

Good Christians do not agree fully on how a person should be baptized. Most agree that baptism is commanded by the Lord. Some sprinkle water on a person's head, others pour the water, and others immerse the person fully in water.

continued on page 110

Please Explain...

What does the Bible teach about how a person should be baptized?

continued from page 109

The word "baptize" literally means to immerse or to dip. there is always enough water around to sprinkle or pour, but several times in the Bible baptism was hindered until there was enough water, evidently so that the person could be fully immersed (See John 3:23 and Acts 8:36-39). Immersion best pictures what God has done in placing us into or immersing us into Christ's invisible body. When the Spirit unites us with Christ, we die with Him and are raised with Him to new life. The action of full immersion also best pictures our own death and resurrection with Christ as we go under the water and come out of it.

One thing is very clear in the Bible: Baptism does not save anyone; it is only a testimony to others that we have been saved. Salvation comes through faith alone in Christ alone. But once someone believes in Christ, they should seek to get baptized to show others they have a new identity as a Christian. All this implies that the person is old enough to understand and believe the gospel, which argues against infant baptism.

Your Turn

6. Have you been baptized? Explain why or why not.

_____

_____

_____

_____

Teach

Again, the essence of discipleship is learning. This requires teaching. But as with Jesus' example, we are not merely to teach doctrinal truths. He said we are to teach people how to "observe," or obey, Christ's commands. This means teaching goes beyond words to our example as models. As it was with Christ and the first disciples, more will probably be caught from our example than taught by our words.

Your Turn

7. Describe how you have taught someone (not just Christian truth, but anything) by word or by example.

_____

_____

_____

_____

Do you think everyone is capable of teaching? Are you? Explain.

_____

_____

_____

_____

Can you now see God's purpose for your life? You are to become active in winning people to Christ and making them into disciples. The more you invest in this purpose, the more your life will reflect God's will. This does not usually mean that you must quit your current job. But you can somehow use that job as a way to reach and teach people about Christ. People might see the way your excellent work and reverent attitude reflect the character of Jesus Christ. This is how God invests eternal significance into even the most mundane or meaningless job. Every job, vocation, or pursuit can be used in this grand purpose for your life.

Your Turn

8. If your purpose in life as a disciple is to help win others to Christ and help them grow as disciples, write down some ways you can do this in your present situation at

home: _____

_____

_____

work: _____

_____

_____

school: _____

_____

_____

neighborhood: _____

_____

_____

What God Wants You to Enjoy

When we submit our lives to God's purpose and learn from Him how to "fish" for people and make them into disciples, we become one of the minority of people on earth who truly understands why we are here. Our reward is the satisfaction that we are doing the work God wants us to do, work that is so important to Him. We are doing something eternally significant with our lives! The Bible tells us that God would like everyone to be saved. He did all He could to accomplish that when He sent His Son to die for all the world. We can continue His purpose by making it our purpose.

Another reward is the knowledge that we are becoming like Jesus Christ. Winning people to Himself was the consuming purpose that drove Jesus to die on the cross. God's heart beats for unsaved people to be saved. When we commit ourselves to evangelism and discipleship, we are near to God's own heart.

Of course, there will also be the satisfaction that we were used to bring a person from eternal death to eternal life, from a future in hell to a future in heaven, from separation from God to the fullness of living with Him.

Finally, there will be the joy of knowing that we have fulfilled our duty as Christians. We have obediently worked to keep The Great Commission. Jesus will be pleased! The Bible even promises a reward that implies a greater experience of glory awaiting us in Christ's kingdom:

Those who are wise shall shine
Like the brightness of the firmament,
And those who turn many to righteousness
Like the stars forever and ever. (Daniel 12:3)

Your Turn

9. What is your strongest motivation for wanting to use your life to bring people to Christ and make them disciples?

_____

_____

_____

_____

Following Christ means that we submissively learn from Him. As a living sacrifice our life is used for the eternal benefit of others. A priority in Jesus' instructions to us is that we should live and speak so as to win people to Christ. This gives us a purpose in life and completes the cycle of discipleship: We win people and disciple them so that they in turn can win others and disciple them. This is God's divine strategy to reach the world through multiplication. And He offers us the opportunity to join Him!

Points to Remember

— God wants you to become a submissive disciple.

— If you submissively follow, Jesus promises that He will make you into someone who will help bring others to Him.

— Jesus commands you to go to people, win them, and make them into disciples.

— This is the highest purpose for your life because it reflects God's own purpose in sending His Son.

❤ Take It to Heart
Memorize these verses:

Matthew 4:19-20 *And He said to them, "Follow Me. and I will make you fishers of men." Then they immediately left their nets and followed Him.*

Matthew 28:18-20 *"All authority has been given to Me in heaven and on earth. Go therefore and make disciples of all the nations, baptizing them in the name of the Father and of the Son and of the Holy Spirit, teaching them to observe all things that I have commanded you; and lo, I am with you always, even to the end of the age."*

Isn't it exciting to realize an eternal purpose for your life? But there is still more that God wants you to know and become. Our next lesson will discuss how God wants you to relate to your possessions.

Lesson 15: Becoming a Generous Disciple

A Look Back
Explain what it means to be a submissive disciple and how you followed God's purpose for your life this past week. Recite the two memory verses from the previous lesson.

_____

_____

_____

A Look Ahead
Disciples generously surrender all their possessions to Jesus Christ.

What God Wants You to Know

Jesus explains another characteristic of a disciple after He gives two hypothetical situations:

"For which of you, intending to build a tower, does not sit down first and count the cost, whether he has enough to finish it; lest, after he has laid the foundation, and is not able to finish, all who see it begin to mock him, saying, 'This man began to build and was not able to finish.' Or what king, going to make war against another king, does not sit down first and consider whether he is able with ten thousand to meet him who comes against him with twenty thousand? Or else, while the other is still a great way off, he sends a delegation and asks conditions of peace. So likewise, whoever of you does not forsake all that he has cannot be My disciple."
(Luke 14:28-33)

Your Turn
1. What similar mistake do the builder and the king make?

_____

_____

How does Jesus apply this to being a disciple?

_____

_____

Living in the Family of Grace

The last verse teaches us that a disciple must "forsake all that he has." Does this mean we should leave everything behind—our possessions, job, home, even our family? To understand what Jesus means, let's look at the two hypothetical situations.

In the first, an unfinished building project teaches that we should "count the cost" before taking on a large and long-term commitment. In the second, a king must count his troops and compare them with the more numerous enemy troops before he decides whether to engage in battle. The issue seems to be the unwillingness or inability to commit everything one has to the cause. In both cases, the failure to consider the cost and consequences of a total commitment of all one's resources would bring ridicule at best and disaster at worst.

The conclusion is then stated: A disciple must forsake all that he has. He knows what the cost of discipleship is, considers his resources, and commits it all to the cause. Imagine a disciple who commits to following a teacher only to discover that more is asked of him than he counted on. He must turn back in shame and embarrassment.

If you are to become a disciple, you must know what the cost is. It is *everything*. Not that you must leave everything, but you must commit everything to God's cause. The issue is ownership. Since a living sacrifice has given all of himself to God, then naturally his possessions are God's too. Who now owns your possessions, your time, your family? You or your Master, the Lord Jesus Christ? A disciple consciously and deliberately turns over to the Lord the ownership of all that he has.

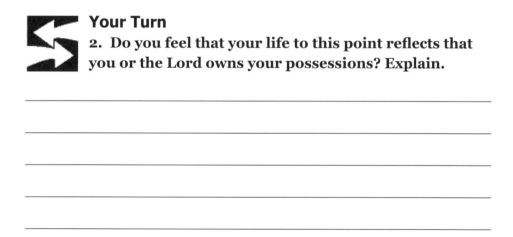

Your Turn
2. Do you feel that your life to this point reflects that you or the Lord owns your possessions? Explain.

_____

_____

_____

_____

_____

God is the rightful Owner of all that we have anyway. He created us and all the things we enjoy. We would have nothing apart from His generosity. However, God entrusts us with His things so that we can use them and manage them for Him. This is called stewardship. A steward is someone given the responsibility of managing another person's property and resources.

These things do not belong to the steward, but to the person who has entrusted them to him. The owner of the property will hold the steward accountable for how he manages it.

We are stewards of God's property. He owns all that we have, but lets us use it. We will one day give an account for how we used it. Also, when God wants to have it back, we must release it. The challenge of discipleship is to be willing to give up whatever God wants when He wants it. We must therefore hold lightly the things we have and learn to practice a generous lifestyle. God wants us to become generous disciples.

The chief responsibility of a steward is explained in the Bible this way: *Moreover it is required in stewards that one be found faithful.*
(1 Corinthians 4:2)

Your Turn
3. What is the chief responsibility of a steward?

_____

_____

_____

What do you think that responsibility involves?

_____

_____

_____

_____

_____

_____

Jesus told a story about three different approaches to stewardship. Consider how each of these stewards handled his master's money:
"For the kingdom of heaven is like a man traveling to a far country, who called his own servants and delivered his goods to them. And to one he gave five talents, to another two, and to another one, to each according to his own ability; and immediately he went on a journey. Then he who had received the five talents went and traded with them, and made another five talents. And likewise he who had received two gained two more also. But he who had received one went and dug in the ground, and hid his lord's money. After a long time the lord of those servants came and settled accounts with them. So he who had received five talents came and brought five other

talents, saying, 'Lord, you delivered to me five talents; look, I have gained five more talents besides them.' His lord said to him, 'Well done, good and faithful servant; you were faithful over a few things, I will make you ruler over many things. Enter into the joy of your lord.' He also who had received two talents came and said, 'Lord, you delivered to me two talents; look, I have gained two more talents besides them.' His lord said to him, 'Well done, good and faithful servant; you have been faithful over a few things, I will make you ruler over many things. Enter into the joy of your lord.' Then he who had received the one talent came and said, 'Lord, I knew you to be a hard man, reaping where you have not sown, and gathering where you have not scattered seed. And I was afraid, and went and hid your talent in the ground. Look, there you have what is yours.' But his lord answered and said to him, 'You wicked and lazy servant, you knew that I reap where I have not sown, and gather where I have not scattered seed. So you ought to have deposited my money with the bankers, and at my coming I would have received back my own with interest. Therefore take the talent from him, and give it to him who has ten talents. For to everyone who has, more will be given, and he will have abundance; but from him who does not have, even what he has will be taken away. And cast the unprofitable servant into the outer darkness. There will be weeping and gnashing of teeth.'" (Matthew 25:14-30)

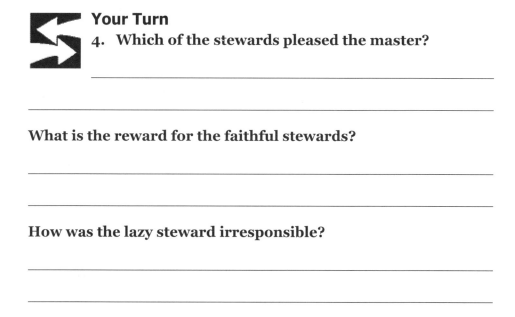

Your Turn

4. Which of the stewards pleased the master?

_____

_____

What is the reward for the faithful stewards?

_____

_____

How was the lazy steward irresponsible?

_____

_____

Our responsibility is to be faithful in managing the resources God gives us. Responsible stewardship means we don't spend it on ourselves, squander it, waste it, or hide it away. Instead we put it to a good use or invest it to increase it.

What we have belongs to God. We are to invest it for Him in things that accomplish His purposes. When we do, He trusts us with more to manage.

What God Wants You to Do

As disciples, we must be willing to give generously from all our possessions, including money. Giving our money is a very important part of our stewardship and our discipleship. God has always expected His people to give their money to His work. In the Old Testament, the Jewish law required the Jewish people to start their giving at ten percent, called a tithe. There were other requirements for giving on top of that. Then they also paid for sacrifices used in worship.

In the New Testament giving money is also expected of Christians, but it is not confined to ten percent. Instead, we read:

So let each one give as he purposes in his heart, not grudgingly or of necessity; for God loves a cheerful giver. (2 Corinthians 9:7)

 Your Turn

5. **What determines our giving according to this verse?**

_____

_____

_____

What attitude should accompany our giving?

_____

_____

_____

Since we are not under the Old Testament law, we don't give "of necessity" or because we have to, but as we determine in our hearts as a response to all that God has done for us. In other words, when we think about God giving His only Son for us, that should motivate us to give back to God. Cheerful giving is generous giving that is not obedience to the law, but a response to grace.

Learning to give back to God will become one of the greatest blessings you have ever experienced.

Your Turn

6. List your major possessions. (Though they are not _possessions_, don't forget your family members that God has entrusted to you).

1.   5.

2.   6.

3.   7.

4.   8.

Now will you consciously and deliberately surrender the ownership of all these things to God? Write out a short deed of ownership assigning it to Him.

_____

_____

_____

_____

_____

_____

_____

_____

_____

Next, write out your commitment to give regularly from your income.

How often will you give? _____

How much will you give? _____

To whom will you give it? _____

What God Wants You to enjoy _____

Please Explain...

How much money should I give?

Since we are no longer under the Old Testament law, some Christians feel a bit lost about how much of their money they should give to God. If we gave as much as the Old Testament law required, we would give about 23% total. But some of that 23% was used to meet social needs that our taxes now supply. There are other examples of those who gave 10% before the law was given.

You might let these figures guide you, but you should not let these figures limit you. As a grateful Christian and steward of God's possessions, you should give whatever expresses your gratitude to God and whatever you believe God wants you to give. As a disciple, you will give generously and sacrificially when you stop to count your blessings, and when you pray and seek God's will about what to give. With such an attitude, giving will not only be generous, but also will be a priority in your budget. Principles for giving under grace (sometimes called "grace-giving") are found in 1 Corinthians 16:1-2 and 2 Corinthians 8 and 9.

When we give we are investing. While we should never give because of what we might get, God does promise a very good return on our investments. God promises abundance here and in eternity.

God promises to meet our needs and to bless us abundantly when we give abundantly. This makes giving a matter of faith. We trust that God will supply our needs and bless us in return for our giving. We see this promise in the verses that both precede and follow the verse we just looked at:

But this I say: He who sows sparingly will also reap sparingly, and he who sows bountifully will also reap bountifully. (2 Corinthians 9:6)

And God is able to make all grace abound toward you, that you, always having all sufficiency in all things, may have an abundance for every good work. (2 Corinthians 9:8)

Your Turn
7. What is promised to those who give generously?

_____

_____

_____

_____

_____

_____

In God's math less is more, and giving means getting. But God does not give us more to make us rich or to spend on ourselves; He gives us more so we can have the blessing of investing more. Note that He gives more grace to us so that we have enough "for every good work." We are channels for God's resources, not receptacles. It is important to understand that God may not always return the blessing in the form of money. There are many ways God can bless us, such as giving us good health that doesn't drain our finances, keeping our car running well, or directing us to a good bargain.

Now you see how giving is really investing. Not only does it bring God's blessings in this life, but Jesus taught that it stores up for us a treasure in eternity:

"Do not lay up for yourselves treasures on earth, where moth and rust destroy and where thieves break in and steal; but lay up for yourselves treasures in heaven, where neither moth nor rust destroys and where

thieves do not break in and steal. For where your treasure is, there your heart will be also." (Matthew 6:19-21)

The form of this treasure in heaven in not explained for us. But does it matter? It is eternal wealth!

This is the reward for the generous disciple. He returns blessings in this life and in the next. You cannot out-give God!

Your Turn
8. What do you think motivates people to give sparingly?

_____

_____

_____

_____

_____

_____

_____

What motivates you to give generously?

_____

_____

_____

_____

_____

_____

_____

God wants us to become generous disciples. We will freely give of our resources when we surrender them to God and act responsibly as stewards. Be thankful for what God allows you to manage, then generously invest it where He leads you.

Points to Remember

— God wants you to become a generous disciple.

— The cost of being a disciple is to surrender all your possessions to Him.

— God owns what you have and lets you manage it as a steward.

— When you give generously, God rewards you with abundance in this life and eternal treasure in the next.

Take It to Heart
Memorize these verses:

Matthew 6:19-21 *"Do not lay up for yourselves treasures on earth, where moth and rust destroy and where thieves break in and steal; but lay up for yourselves treasures in heaven, where neither moth nor rust destroys and where thieves do not break in and steal. For where your treasure is, there your heart will be also."*

There is now only one more characteristic of a disciple that you need to learn about. Please go on to the last lesson.